MUMMY

Arrowheads from Egyptian sand grave, c. 3000 B.C.

Slate palette from Egyptian grave, c. 3000 B.C.

Gold ear spools from ancient Peruvian grave

Chancay pottery figure from a Peruvian burial

Peruvian doll buried with mummy

Case for mummy of shrew mouse, Egyptian, c. 600 B.C.

Ancient Egyptian canopic jars, to hold internal organs of sacred Apis Bull (left) and person (right)

Peruvian pot from grave

DK Eyewitness Books

Wooden figure of Anubis, the ancient Egyptian god of embalming

Hand from ancient Egyptian mummy with individually wrapped fingers

MUMMY

Written by
JAMES PUTNAM

Photographed by
PETER HAYMAN

Wooden face from ancient Egyptian mummy case

Magical amulets with heads of four Sons of Horus

Dorling Kindersley

Flint knife found in ancient Egyptian grave, c. 3000 B.C.

Fist amulet

Head from Egyptian mummy

Dorling Kindersley

LONDON, NEW YORK, AUCKLAND, DELHI, JOHANNESBURG, MUNICH,
PARIS and SYDNEY

For a full catalog, visit

DK www.dk.com

Project editor Scott Steedman
Art editor Bob Gordon
Managing editor Helen Parker
Managing art editor Julia Harris
Production Louise Barratt
Picture research Cynthia Hole
Editorial consultants The Department of
Egyptian Antiquities, British Museum

This Eyewitness ® Book has been conceived by
Dorling Kindersley Limited and Editions Gallimard

© 1993 Dorling Kindersley Limited
This edition © 2000 Dorling Kindersley Limited
First American edition, 1993

Published in the United States by
Dorling Kindersley Publishing, Inc.
95 Madison Avenue
New York, NY 10016
4 6 8 10 9 7 5

Dorling Kindersley books are available at special discounts for bulk purchases for sales
promotions or premiums. Special editions, including personalized covers, excerpts of
existing guides, and corporate imprints can be created in large quantities for specific
needs. For more information, contact Special Markets Dept., Dorling Kindersley
Publishing, Inc., 95 Madison Ave., New York, NY 10016; Fax: (800) 600-9098

Library of Congress Cataloging-in-Publication Data
Putnam, James.
Mummy / written by James Putnam.
p. cm. — (Eyewitness Books)
Includes index.
Summary: Documents the history and significance of mummies, both natural and
man-made, and describes the principles and ceremonies associated with them.
1. Mummies — Juvenile literature. [1. Mummies.] I. Title.
GT3340.P87 2000 393'.3 — dc20 92-1591
ISBN 0-7894-5857-8 (pb)
ISBN 0-7894-5856-X (hc)

Color reproduction by Colourscan, Singapore
Printed in China by Toppan Printing Co. (Shenzhen) Ltd.

Chimu mummy bundle
from ancient Peru

Gilded wooden coffin
of ancient Egyptian
priestess, c. 1250 B.C.

Contents

Egyptian pot containing
linen mummy bandages,
c. 2000 B.C.

What are mummies?

Mummies are the preserved bodies of people or animals. The word was first used to describe the bandaged bodies of ancient Egyptians. But any dead body that still has skin on it is a mummy. If people die or are buried in the right conditions, they may be mummified (preserved) by accident (pp. 8–9). This can happen in wet, marshy places (pp. 58–59) or in the freezing cold of mountains or the polar regions. But most often, people are preserved by being dried out. Many cultures have developed a chemical process – called embalming – to achieve this artificially. The ancient Egyptians are famous for their skillful embalming and their elaborate burial customs. But people all over the world have embalmed their dead. Wherever it is practiced, mummification is usually done for religious reasons. Most cultures believe in some kind of afterlife (life after death). By preserving a dead person's body in recognizable form, they hope to prepare him or her for a better future life.

STUFFED ANIMALS
Unlike mummies, stuffed animals are usually little more than dried skin complete with feathers or fur. The taxidermist props this up with a wire framework to make a lifelike animal.

WHY MUMMY?
Egyptian mummies were coated in dark resins. When Arabs invaded Egypt in the 7th century A.D., they thought this was bitumen (asphalt) and called them *mummiya* – Arabic for bitumen.

OUR LEADER
Famous people are sometimes mummified. The Russian revolutionary leader Vladimir Lenin was preserved using a secret technique that involved paraffin wax. Millions of communists have traveled to Moscow to see his body lying in state in Red Square.

ALL WRAPPED UP
This is one of the earliest ancient Egyptian mummies, from 2400 B.C. Egyptian mummies are often carefully wrapped in hundreds of feet of linen bandages (pp. 16–17).

False beard

INTO THE AFTERLIFE
The Egyptians believed that a person's soul left the body at death (pp. 12–13). After the burial, the soul was reunited with the body, and the mummy lived on in the afterlife. For all this to happen, the body had to be well preserved. Then it was bandaged and laid in a coffin or mummy case. The technique of embalming developed gradually over ancient Egypt's long history. It reached its peak around 1000 B.C., but Romans living in Egypt were still being mummified in the third century A.D. (pp. 42–43). This well-wrapped mummy of a 50-year-old man probably dates from the Late Period, between 1085 and 305 B.C. (p. 10).

Mummy wrapped in linen bandages

Base of mummy case

MUMMIFIED BUDDHA

Certain Buddhist priests in Japan had a tradition of mummification. The mummies were set up in temples, where they were worshiped like statues. The priests who became mummies were given the title *Nikushin-butsu*, which means "a Buddha of the body." This is the priest Tetsumonkai. He participated in his own mummification by eating a special grain-free diet for the three years before he died, in 1829. Then the other priests smoke-dried his body with huge candles.

Hooded parka made of sealskin

STOPPING THE ROT

Ancient Egyptian embalmers realized that a body's internal organs were the first to decay. So they removed the lungs, liver, stomach, and intestines through an incision in the left side (pp. 14–15). The brain was usually extracted through the nose. The empty body could then be dried out by covering it in natron, a naturally occurring salt. Embalm literally means "in balsam," a sweet-smelling oil. After they had been dried, Egyptian mummies were coated in ointments, oils, and resins, to keep the skin supple and lifelike.

Mummy case lid

Painted figures of gods

NICE HAIR

This skull from a female Egyptian mummy dates from around 1600 B.C. As sometimes happens, the flesh has decayed but the tougher hair has been preserved.

THE MUMMY'S HOUSE

Egyptian mummies were usually buried in tombs. In the Old Kingdom (2686–2160 B.C.), the pharaohs (Egyptian kings) built pyramid tombs. These are the famous pyramids at Giza. The largest of the three, the Great Pyramid of Khufu, was made of 2,300,000 blocks of stone and stands 480 ft (146 m) high. Because the mummies were buried inside with many treasures, the pyramids were robbed in ancient times.

GOLDEN PHARAOH

Probably the best known pharaoh is Tutankhamun (pp. 38–39). He was not an important ruler, but his intact tomb, found in 1922, was crammed with beautiful treasures. This is his mummy mask, made of solid gold. Compared to that of many pharaohs, his mummy was in poor condition.

ESKIMO BOY

This six-month-old Inuit (Eskimo) boy died around 1475. He is one of eight well-preserved mummies discovered on a jagged cliff in Greenland in 1972. Following Inuit tradition, he had been dressed in warm clothes and left with objects to help him in the next world. Protected from the sun and snow by a rocky overhang, the boy's body was slowly freeze-dried by the cold Arctic air (p. 63).

Natural mummies

Flint knife buried in sand with body

SOME OF THE MOST REMARKABLE MUMMIES have been preserved by accident. Natural mummies are usually found in extreme climates where dry sands or freezing cold have somehow stopped the process of decay. Decay is caused by bacteria, which breed in the water that makes up over 70 percent of a person's body weight. Hot desert sands can preserve a body by dehydrating it (drying it out). Bodies buried in the icy polar regions may be so thoroughly frozen that decay never starts. Occasionally, bodies have been freeze-dried by a combination of cold temperatures and very dry winds, as found in some mountain caves (pp. 7, 63). In northern Europe, the unusual conditions found in marshy bogs have also preserved bodies remarkably well.

GRAVE GOODS
All over the world, the dead are buried with beautiful objects. They are usually put there for religious reasons. This 5,000-year-old pot was part of a sand burial. It was meant to hold food the dead person would need in the afterlife.

Dry skin stretched tightly over skeleton

Knees pulled up against chest

SAND MUMMY
The earliest surviving Egyptian mummies date from around 3200 B.C. This is just before the first written records, so very little is known about them. The dead person was placed in a simple grave that was little more than a shallow oval dug in the desert sand. The body lay in a crouched position, with the head to the south and the face turned to the west, toward the setting sun. It was then covered in sand, which mummified it naturally. The many objects buried with the "sand mummies" show that the Egyptians already believed in life after death. The rough graves must have been soon lost in the desert's moving sands, and uncovering such lifelike bodies by accident may have encouraged the Egyptians' beliefs. The most famous sand mummy is nicknamed "Ginger" because of his red hair. This female mummy, also in the British Museum, is known as "Gingerella."

Slate palette in shape of turtle

Necklaces of beads and shells

ADORNING THE BODY
The most curious items found with sand burials were slate palettes. They were used to grind up make-up, and also had an unknown magical function. Necklaces of beads and shells have also been found.

BODY CAST

Over 2,000 ancient Romans died in A.D. 79, in a huge eruption of Mount Vesuvius that engulfed the town of Pompeii. The volcanic ash set around their bodies like wet cement. Over the years, the bodies decayed, and the ash turned to solid rock. A perfect mold of the body shape survived. When the ruins of Pompeii were excavated, these body hollows were discovered and a method of filling them with liquid plaster was developed. This created a perfect replica of the dead person, like a mummy with flesh of plaster.

Trace of clothing wrapped around body

TOLLUND MAN

This is the head of a man discovered in the Tollund Bog in Denmark in 1950. He has been dead for more than 2,000 years, but looks like he is just sleeping. He was found with a noose around his neck; he is thought to have been sacrificed and thrown into the bog as part of a spring fertility ritual (pp. 58–59).

Noose

Sheepskin cap tied under the chin

Stubble, thought to be two or three days' growth

ICY GRAVE

This is John Torrington, one of three well-preserved mummies discovered by scientists in the Canadian Arctic in 1984. They were English sailors who had died on Sir John Franklin's tragic expedition to find the Northwest Passage. Franklin left England with two ships in 1845, and was never seen again. "It's as if he's just unconscious," marveled one of the scientists as he lifted Torrington from his icy coffin.

BUILDER'S SACRIFICE

Mummies of animals are sometimes found in ordinary houses. Cold drafts of air may freeze-dry the bodies of mice that die in walls or under floorboards. In 16th- and 17th-century England, builders who had almost finished a house used to place a dead animal in a nook somewhere and board it up with a few lucky items. This is a mummified chicken, found behind a brick wall in a 17th-century house in London.

A land lost in time

THE ANCIENT EGYPTIANS went to great lengths to preserve their bodies and their worldly possessions. This has helped the world to rediscover ancient Egypt. The civilization of the pharaohs flourished by the Nile River for over 3,000 years. But until the French invaded Egypt in 1798, it had been virtually forgotten. The travelers who visited the country were amazed by its ancient monuments and tombs covered in mysterious hieroglyphics (picture-writing). People have been reopening tombs in search of treasures since ancient times. But until recently, they paid little attention to the mummies. We now know that with the help of modern science, these timeless bodies can tell us amazing things about life and death in ancient times.

LANDS OF THE NILE
Egypt is mostly desert, and life has always been concentrated along the banks of the Nile River. In ancient times the land was often divided in two. The northern part, which included the fertile Nile Delta, was called Lower Egypt. In the south was Upper Egypt, which included a large area now flooded by the huge Aswan Dam.

Texture of tight linen bandages impressed on skin

OLD KING'S TOMB
The period we call ancient Egypt began around 3000 B.C. The step pyramid at Saqqara was built c. 2650 B.C., in the Old Kingdom. This was followed by the Middle and New Kingdoms, the Late Period, and then an era when Egypt was ruled by the Greeks and later the Romans.

TOMB GUARD
Beautiful statues were placed in tombs for religious reasons. This painted wooden statue represents the god Anubis. He has the head of a jackal, or wild dog. Anubis was the god of mummification and guardian of the cemeteries.

NEST FOR A MUMMY
After it was embalmed and wrapped, the mummy was laid in a coffin. This might be the first in a whole series (or nest) of mummy cases. The Egyptians believed these cases would magically protect the body. They were covered in elaborate paintings and spells to help the mummy's spirit on its difficult path through the afterlife.

FAMILIAR FACE?
The ancient Egyptians took extra care preserving the features of the face. This was because they believed the dead person's spirit had to return to the tomb and recognize its body before the mummy could live forever (pp. 12–13).

NAPOLEON MEETS A MUMMY
The French were the first Europeans to study ancient Egypt seriously. When Napoleon Bonaparte invaded Egypt in 1798, he brought a team of scholars and artists with him. Napoleon was fascinated by the ancient land and collected several mummies himself.

ANCIENT LIVES
The ancient Egyptians decorated the walls of tombs with beautiful paintings that tell us a lot about their everyday lives. Paintings that show people farming, hunting, feasting, relaxing, and attending religious and royal ceremonies have all been found.

MUMMY TRADE
Excavating in Egypt's hot, dusty climate is tiring. This is a dig in the 1900s. By then, mummies could be sold for a high price. In the 16th and 17th centuries, they were ground up and used in medicines (p. 40). Local people also used them as fuel, as they are soaked in resins and burn well.

FATHER OF EGYPTOLOGY
It took the French scholar Jean-François Champollion (1790–1832) most of his life to decipher hieroglyphics. He announced his first breakthrough in 1822. This allowed Egyptologists, scientists who study ancient Egypt, to read the inscriptions on statues, tombs, temples, and mummy cases.

Idealized image of dead person

Wig

Elaborate collar

Beetle god holding sun

Opening page of *The Description of Egypt*, published from 1809 to 1822 by the team of scholars that went with Napoleon.

TIME CAPSULE
Inside the wrappings of this mummy is a middle-aged Roman man. X-rays show that he suffered from arthritis of the spine (pp. 48–51).

Spell for dead person's soul written in hieroglyphics

Winged gods

Ankh, symbol of life

STRANGE SYMBOLS
Mummy cases are covered in religious symbols meant to help the dead person. Only when they could read hieroglyphics could Egyptologists begin to make sense of the Egyptians' complex religious beliefs. The writings often give the name and title of the dead person and sometimes his or her father or mother, too.

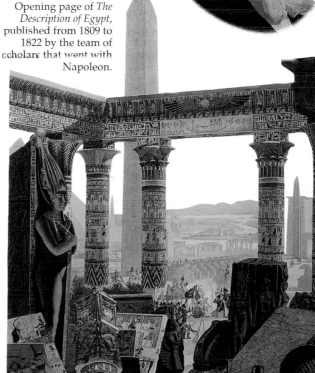

The Egyptian Book of the Dead

IT'S CALLED A BOOK, but the Egyptian Book of the Dead is really a collection of magic spells. By about 1400 B.C., they were usually written on a roll of papyrus, the Egyptians' form of paper. There were over 200 spells, which the Egyptians called "The Spells for Coming Forth by Day." Each spell was a prayer or a plea from the dead person, and was meant to help on the difficult voyage to the next world. The ancient Egyptians believed every person had several spirit forms, the most important being the *Ka* and the *Ba*. The *Ka* was the vital energy of life. Like any living thing, the *Ka* needed food and drink, which the Egyptians provided through offerings or images of food placed in the tomb (p. 31). A person's character and ability to move around was called its *Ba*. The *Ba* is something like our idea of a person's spirit or soul, and was usually pictured as a bird. For a person to live forever, his or her *Ba* and *Ka* had to be reunited in the tomb with the mummy. Once this happened, the mummy became an immortal (or *Akh*).

HARD-WORKING SPELL
Shabti figures (pp. 32–33) are painted with a spell promising they will work for the dead person in the afterlife.

GOLD HEART
This gold heart scarab is an amulet (pp. 20–21) worn by the mummy for protection. It is inscribed with a spell to help the heart when it was weighed (p. 13). An ancient papyrus records that robbers brought to trial in 1125 B.C. confessed that they had stolen it from the tomb of Pharaoh Sobkemsaf II.

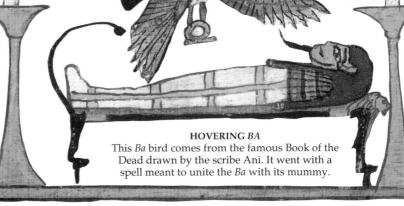

HOVERING *BA*
This *Ba* bird comes from the famous Book of the Dead drawn by the scribe Ani. It went with a spell meant to unite the *Ba* with its mummy.

FIRST BOOKS
In the Old Kingdom, over 4,000 years ago, magic spells were inscribed on the inner walls of pyramids. By the Middle Kingdom, they were painted inside coffins, like this one from 2000 B.C. The first Book of the Dead on papyrus dates from around 1400 B.C.

RISE, MUMMY!
Ba birds have human heads. This little statue was probably originally attached to the foot of a mummy case. The *Ba* is raising its arms, as if it is telling the mummy's spirit to rise. Two outstretched human arms were the hieroglyphic symbol for the *Ka*.

Forked tool used to touch mummy's face

Set of tools used in the Opening of the Mouth

Adz, a tool held up to mummy's face

OPEN UP
During the funeral, the mummy went through an important ritual called the Opening of the Mouth. The ancient Egyptians believed this would restore the mummy's senses, so it could eat, drink, and enjoy the afterlife properly. This illustration is from the Book of the Dead by the scribe Hunefer, from c. 1310 B.C.

Priest in leopard skin burning incense

Food offerings

Priests

Mummy

Mourners

JACKAL HEAD
This Anubis mask has a moving jaw. It may have been worn by a priest during rituals like the Opening of the Mouth.

Priest wearing Anubis mask

Jury of gods sits in judgment

God Osiris

WEIGHING THE HEART
The most important moment in a mummy's "life" was the weighing of its heart. In this ceremony, a jury of gods decided whether the mummy had behaved well enough on earth to deserve eternal life. This was calculated by weighing the mummy's heart against a feather, the symbol of truth. The jackal god Anubis performed the ceremony, and Thoth, the scribe god, took notes. If sins on Earth had made the mummy's heart too heavy, it was thrown to the monster Ammit, who devoured it. But if the heart balanced with the Feather of Truth, the mummy had passed the test and would live forever.

Dead man watches anxiously with wife

Ba bird

Heart

Anubis, the jackal god, keeps eye on scales

Feather of Truth

Thoth, the scribe god, writes down result

Monster Ammit with crocodile's head waits to devour heart

BOOK HOLDER
This wooden statue of Osiris, the god of rebirth (pp. 34–35), was placed in a tomb. It has a secret compartment where the Book of the Dead was hidden.

Roll of papyrus

Base

Secret compartment

EGYPTIAN PAPER
The scribes, ancient Egypt's full-time writers, usually copied the Book of the Dead onto papyrus. This reed used to grow in marshes by the Nile. Strips of papyrus were woven together and beaten to form long rolls like paper.

Making a mummy

Wooden jackal, representing Anubis, the god of embalming

"MY CORPSE IS PERMANENT, it will not perish nor be destroyed in this land for ever." So ends spell 154 in the Book of the Dead (pp. 12–13).

From the earliest sand burials 5,000 years ago (p. 8), the Egyptians could see that a body had to be dried to stop it from rotting away. They developed a method of drying with natron, a natural salt that left a corpse more flexible and lifelike than drying with hot sand. Natron absorbs water. It also dissolves body fats, and is a mild antiseptic that kills destructive bacteria. Embalming traditionally took 70 days, of which 40 used to dry the body. But first of all the vital organs, which decay the fastest, had to be removed. Only the heart, which the mummy would need when it was judged in the next world (p. 13), was left. The body was then washed with palm wine and spices and covered in natron. Later, molten (liquid) resin, taken from trees, was poured over the body to help preserve it. To stop it from cracking, the skin was rubbed with a mixture of cedar oil, wax, natron, and gum. Then the body was packed with wads of linen, sand, or even sawdust, to give it shape. Finally the mummy was ready to be wrapped in layers of linen bandages.

EMBALMING EYEWITNESS
The Greek historian Herodotus visited Egypt in 450 B.C. and wrote the only eyewitness account of embalming. "In the best treatment," he observed, "first of all they draw out the brains through the nostrils with an iron hook…. Next they make an incision in the flank with a sharp obsidian blade through which they can extract all the internal organs. Then they clean out the body cavity, rinsing it with palm wine…(then) they cover the corpse with natron for seventy days, but for no longer, and so mummify it. After the seventy days are up they wash the corpse and wrap it from head to toe in bandages of the finest linen anointed with gum."

FOUR DUMMIES
The mummy's internal organs were embalmed separately. By about 2000 B.C., they were placed in containers called canopic jars. These little coffins had heads, either of gods or the dead person. By 1000 B.C., the wrapped organs were put back in the mummy. But dummy canopic jars with nothing in them were still put in the tomb. These dummy jars have the heads of the four gods known as the Sons of Horus (p. 20).

Imsety, with a person's head, guarded the liver

Qebehsenuef, a falcon, held the intestines

Hapy, a baboon, kept an eye on the lungs

Duamutef, a jackal, guarded the stomach

Body / Embalmers pour water from jugs

Body, black from oils and resins, is purified with streams of water

Embalmers / Head embalmer wearing Anubis mask

Lying on bier (couch), body is covered in dry crystals of natron

CANOPIC CHEST
This wooden chest belonged to a doctor called Gua, who died c. 2050 B.C. It contains his four canopic jars. They have human heads – it wasn't until 1500 B.C. that the Sons of Horus (p. 20) became common as stoppers.

Wooden stoppers

Jars made of the stone calcite

BRAIN HOOKS
A rod was usually pushed up the nose to punch a hole into the skull. Then bronze hooks or spoons could be poked in to scoop out the brain.

Head support

Embalming incision

BOWL OF NATRON
A natural salt, natron was found around the edges of desert lakes near Cairo.

Wax embalming plate with wedjat-eye decoration

Ritual knife with gold handle and flint blade

EMBALMING TOOLS
The embalming incision was usually made on the left side of the body. Herodotus says the knife blade was made of obsidian, a kind of volcanic glass that had to be imported from Ethiopia. But all the ritual knives that have been found have blades of flint. After the organs had been removed, the incision was covered by a plate decorated with a wedjat eye (p. 20).

WHERE THE SUN SETS...
Cemeteries, tombs, and embalmers' workshops were usually on the west bank of the Nile. The Egyptians believed this desert area where the sun set every evening was the land of the dead.

STEP BY STEP
The best pictures of embalming are painted on the mummy case of Djedbastiufankh, from about 600 B.C. This case is now in the Hildesheim Museum, Germany.

Wrapped mummy

Canopic jars

Mummy, bandaged and wearing a mask (pp. 18–19), is attended by Anubis

WELL PRESERVED
Considering that she was mummified after 600 B.C., around the time Herodotus visited Egypt, this woman has been remarkably well embalmed. By then, the empire was collapsing and the art of embalming was in decline. Embalmers still made sure the mummy looked good on the outside, but they didn't bother much with the insides. Usually bodies were simply coated from head to toe in resin.

Wrapping up

NEED A HAND?
Each finger on this 3,000-year-old mummified hand has been individually wrapped. It is wearing a gold ring set with a scarab beetle (p. 44). Rings and other jewelry were often specially made just to be worn by mummies.

HUNDREDS OF YARDS OF LINEN were used to carefully wrap a mummy. The linen didn't just come in the well-known rolls of bandages. Mummies were also wrapped in shrouds, large sheets of material that were thrown over the body like a cape. Each shroud had to be long enough to be knotted at the top, behind the mummy's head, and also underneath the feet. As many as 20 alternating layers of bandages and shrouds have been counted on one mummy. The exact arrangement of the rolls and shrouds of linen varied a lot from period to period, and can be helpful in dating mummies. The first layer was usually a shroud. Then each finger and toe was wrapped up separately. Next a long strip of linen beginning at the right shoulder was crisscrossed over the head. To hold the head up, a strap was then passed under the chin and knotted on top of the head. As more bandages were added, they were kept very tight, to maintain the mummy's distinctive shape. Protective amulets (pp. 20–21) and sometimes the dead person's jewelry were placed between the layers. At the same time the linen was constantly brushed with sticky, liquid resin. This glued the bandages together and made them slowly stiffen as they dried. Around 15 days were set aside for the wrapping, and the whole process was accompanied by much prayer and ritual.

THE FINAL SHROUD
The wrapping was completed by a shroud. This covered the entire mummy and was held in place by a long bandage running from head to toe and crossed by horizontal bands.

Inscription in hieroglyphic

SHROUD FRAGMENT
Numbers had many meanings to the ancient Egyptians. Traditionally, mummies were wrapped in seven shrouds, as this was a magical number. The outer shroud was often painted with magical writings and spells to protect the mummy within.

IT'S A WRAP
In this imaginative picture of a wrapping, an assistant is busy pouring the resin used to hold the bandages together. Lying on a special bier (couch), the mummy is being wrapped in stages, supervised by the chief embalmer. Priests kneel at the feet of the mummy, reciting sacred spells. In the background, more assistants are trying to get the mummy case (pp. 22–27) down the stairs.

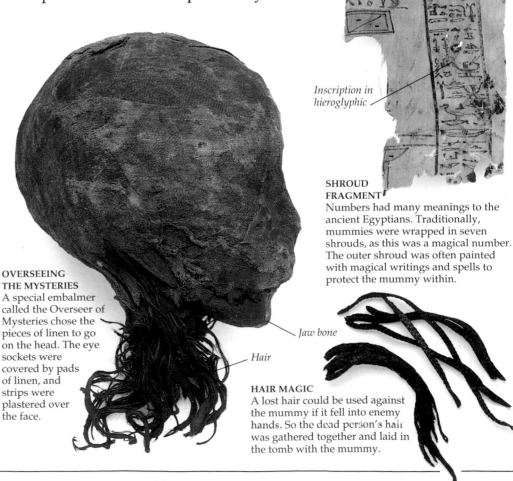

OVERSEEING THE MYSTERIES
A special embalmer called the Overseer of Mysteries chose the pieces of linen to go on the head. The eye sockets were covered by pads of linen, and strips were plastered over the face.

Jaw bone

Hair

HAIR MAGIC
A lost hair could be used against the mummy if it fell into enemy hands. So the dead person's hair was gathered together and laid in the tomb with the mummy.

Final
shroud

Writing used
to date linen

LINEN OF YESTERDAY
All the wrappings above were unrolled from the
same mummy. The linen varies a lot in quality. The
cheapest was old household cloth. This explains a sad
Egyptian funeral song in which the dead person is said to be
sleeping in the "cast-off linen of yesterday." This domestic
linen is well worn and has often been darned. The best
mummy wrappings were clothes used to dress
statues of gods in the temples. Writing on
wrappings can be used to date mummies.

A French archaeologist
discovers a mummy in the
ruins of Antinoe, 1896

ROMAN BOY
Inside these wrappings is the body
of a Roman boy. X-rays show that
he was about eight when he died.
He is lying with his hands by his
sides and is wearing a bracelet
on his right wrist.

TOOTSIES
Even the toenails on this
beautifully bandaged foot have
been individually wrapped.

Mummy masks

A BEAUTIFUL MASK did more than protect the mummy's face – it could also act as a substitute head if the mummy's real head was lost or damaged. When the dead person's spirit (the *Ba*, p. 12) returned to the tomb, it could recognize the mummy by its mask. One of the most famous works of art in the world is the stunning gold mask found on Tutankhamun's mummy (pp. 7, 39). The masks of pharaohs may all have been made of solid gold, often inlaid with beautiful gemstones. The use of gold was connected to the belief that the sun god, with whom the mummy hoped to be united, had flesh of pure gold. Less important mummies wore masks made from cartonnage, a sort of paper-mâché of linen or scrap papyrus gummed together with plaster or resin. The wet cartonnage was molded to fit the mummy. Once it had hardened, it could then be gilded (covered in gold leaf) or painted in rich colors.

Floral wreath

Gold earrings

Bead necklace

Winged scarab beetle

ALL DRESSED UP FOR THE AFTERLIFE
This Roman mummy mask shows a woman dressed in her best clothes and wearing her favorite jewelry. She is even wearing make-up so she will look her best for the gods.

Sacred flower

Bracelet

Gold headdress with wings of a vulture

Striped wig

FIT FOR A PRINCESS
This cartonnage mask from about 1900 B.C. belonged to a wealthy woman. She has not been identified, but the beautiful vulture headdress she is wearing suggests that she may have been a princess.

Prayer to Osiris to provide food

Prayer to Anubis for a good burial

Raised relief coated in gold

GREEK GOLD
Cartonnage mummy masks were particularly popular by Greek and Roman times (pp. 42–43). This elegant gilded mask is rich in raised decoration, a typical feature of the period.

Floral wreath

Curly wig

SPITTING IMAGE
Ancient Egyptian masks were usually idealized, with perfect features and a calm and noble expression. Greek mummies (pp. 42–43) wore more personal masks with realistic features and vividly painted details. These masks seem to represent real people.

WOODEN FEATURES
This mask was carved from wood and then painted. It comes from 1350 B.C. – the same period in which Tutankhamun was pharaoh (pp. 38–39).

Pierced ears for wearing studs

Collar of lotus petals

Linen strips holding mask and pectoral in place

Pectoral, a painted cartonnage chest decoration

TIED DOWN
After the careful embalming and wrapping processes, the mask was finally fitted over the mummy's head. It was then lashed in place with more bandages. Often a decorated pectoral (chest plate) and foot case (p. 27) were added in the same way.

Eye of Horus (wedjat)

Ba (soul) bird

EVERY PICTURE TELLS A STORY
This cartonnage mask from the Roman period is gilded and painted with many religious scenes. Glass eyes were added to create a more lifelike appearance.

Gods holding the Feather of Truth

Amulets and magic charms

ANCIENT EGYPTIANS WORE AMULETS, or charms, after they died, just as they did in life. They believed these charms had magical properties to protect the body from evil or bring good luck. Many different kinds of amulets, often representing plants, animals, or parts of the body, were placed inside a mummy's wrappings. Several hundred amulets have been found on a single mummy. They were positioned on the body according to the Book of the Dead (pp. 12–13), and many were inscribed with excerpts from these sacred writings. The particular stone or material used for the amulet was believed to give it extra power. Priests often spoke spells and prayers as the sacred amulets were placed on the mummy.

Clenched fist, to give power of action

Two finger amulet laid on embalming incision

THE THREE GRACES
Between them, the mother goddess Isis (right), her son Horus (center), and her sister Nephthys (left) gave powerful overall protection to the mummy.

EYE OF HORUS
According to an ancient legend, the god Horus had his eye miraculously restored after he had lost it in a fight with evil. This eye symbol, known as the wedjat eye, became connected to healing. It was thought to protect the mummy's health and give the body new vitality.

Taweret

Bes

ODD COUPLE
Taweret the pregnant hippopotamus was the goddess of childbirth. Her lion-maned assistant, Bes, was a dwarf who protected women and children.

FOUR SONS OF HORUS
These amulets guarded the vital organs, usually removed and placed in canopic jars (pp. 14–15). They are made from faience, a type of glazed pottery.

Imsety
(human head)

Duamutef
(jackal head)

Qebehsenuef
(falcon head)

Hapy
(baboon head)

HEAD WARMER
This bronze disc was tucked under a mummy's head. It carried a spell meant to keep the head warm.

Plaited wig

Real rings

Stone ear studs

Gilded mask

Headrest amulet made of obsidian

Wooden arms

Wooden arms

20

Scarab beetle

Holes for sewing into bandages

Beetle's wings, made of faience

WINGED HEART SCARAB
Egyptians thought that intelligence dwelled in the heart, not the brain. This heart amulet made sure that the mummy went into the afterlife with all of his or her wits intact.

Falcon head

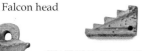

STAIRWAY TO HEAVEN
These steps symbolize the stairs on Osiris' throne, which every mummy's spirit would have to climb (pp. 34-35).

Papyrus reed (p. 13)

Heart, made from a red-and-white stone called breccia

Heart scarab

Scarab beetle

Girdle of Isis

CLOSE TO THE MUMMY'S HEART
This heart scarab has no wings. These important amulets were often set in a frame and sewn on top of the mummy's wrappings. The ancient Egyptians thought that the scarab beetle (p. 44) was born magically from a ball of dung. So it was not surprising that they associated it with rebirth after death. A spell from the Book of the Dead that would help in the Weighing of the Heart (p. 13) was written on the other side of the amulet.

GIRDLE OF ISIS
This knot amulet represents Isis, the mother goddess. It is made of red stone, to represent her blood. Placed on the chest, the girdle was a powerful symbol that protected the mummy.

Head of a lioness

Weight, made of blue faience

Shen, a circle of cord, a symbol of completeness and eternity

Plaque showing Anubis

Shabti figure

WELL PROTECTED
The upper part of the body usually received most of the amulets, with many grouped around the heart or just below the waist. This female mummy is protected by a fine selection of amulets – though most are still hidden among her bandages. She is also wearing some of her favorite jewelry.

Nut, the sky goddess, wrapping her wings around the mummy

Outer mummy
case base

Inner mummy
case base

Mummy cover
(top and bottom)

Outer mummy case lid

Inner mummy
case lid

Gilded
top half

Wedjat
eyes

Painted
wood

Wood completely
covered in gold

A MUMMY'S NEST
This nest of mummy cases was made for
Henutmehit, a priestess in the Egyptian capital of Thebes
around 1250 B.C. The fine gold decoration suggests that she was
very important. Her mummy, which has not been found, would have
been protected by the mummy cover. This has an upper and lower
part, both made of cartonnage. The mummy was then laid into two
wooden cases, with the inner case fitting inside the outer one. Both
have eyes and eyebrows made of a black volcanic glass called obsidian.

Mummy cases

AFTER AN ANCIENT EGYPTIAN HAD BEEN EMBALMED and bandaged, his or her body was placed in a coffin or mummy case. The case protected the mummy from wild animals and tomb thieves. More importantly, it was regarded as a substitute body and a house for the dead person's spirit. Mummy cases changed a lot through ancient Egypt's long history. The first ones were usually just plain rectangular wooden boxes. By the Middle Kingdom, about 2000 B.C., wealthy people were being placed inside two mummy cases for extra protection. Around the same time, the first mummiform (mummy-shaped) cases began to appear. By the New Kingdom, from 1567 to 1085 B.C., both inner and outer mummiform coffins were popular.

EARLY MUMMY CASE
About 5,000 years ago, an ancient Egyptian was placed in this reed basket and buried in the hot sand. Like a sand mummy (p. 8), he or she was laid in a hunched-up position with the knees tucked up by the face. But the basket stopped the sand from preserving the body, so only a skeleton remains.

FINISHING TOUCHES
This painting comes from the walls of the tomb of Ipuy, a sculptor during the reign of Ramesses the Great (pp. 36, 50). It shows workers putting the finishing touches on Ipuy's wooden mummy cases.

FACING THE RISING SUN
A masked man called Ankhef lies in his rectangular coffin from around 2020 B.C. At some point he must have been turned around, because he should be lying on his left side, with his head on the headrest, which is now by his feet. Mummies often faced east, so they could see the sun, a symbol of rebirth, rise over the desert each morning.

Body wrapped in shroud   *Headrest*

WRAPPED IN FEATHERS
A vulture's feathers protect the owner of this mummy case lid. It is known as a *rishi* case, from the Arabic word for feathered.

PAINTED EYES
False eyes were painted on the east side of this wooden inner coffin (c. 2000 B.C.). Lying on its side, the mummy could "look out" through the eyes. Below them is a painted door, for the mummy's spirit to leave and reenter the coffin.

False eyes

False door

23

Continued on next page

Outer coffin lid   Inner coffin   Masked mummy   Unwrapped mummy

TINY NEST FOR A TINY MUMMY
This is one of two tiny nests of coffins found among all the treasures in Tutankhamun's tomb (pp. 38–39). It contained the mummified body of an unborn child, probably the king's daughter. The wrapped mummy was wearing a mask and lying inside a gilded inner coffin. All this fit inside a second, outer coffin less than 19.5 inches (50 cm) long.

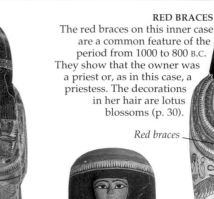

RED BRACES
The red braces on this inner case are a common feature of the period from 1000 to 800 B.C. They show that the owner was a priest or, as in this case, a priestess. The decorations in her hair are lotus blossoms (p. 30).

Red braces

MUMMY CARGO
This tomb sculpture shows a mummy making the symbolic journey to Abydos, the city of the god Osiris (pp. 34–35).

Sandaled feet

Wooden case of the priestess Katebet, c. 1300 B.C.

SEX CHANGE
This coffin's pink face shows that it was made for a woman. But the inscription says the owner was a man, an official called Nesperennub, who lived around 800 B.C. Egyptians often took over other people's coffins in this way.

Why cartonnage?

Wood was the ideal material for making mummy cases. But there are very few large trees in Egypt, and the best pieces of wood had to be imported. An excellent alternative was cartonnage (p. 18), which was cheap, light, and easy to shape and paint.

OFF TO FRANCE
Napoleon's army (pp. 10–11) removed many mummy cases from their tombs and carried them back to France. Most are now in the Louvre Museum in Paris.

MAGIC SYMBOLS
The symbols painted on cases were meant to protect the mummy or help it on the difficult voyage to the afterlife. Apart from gods and magic symbols, decoration included floral wreaths, elaborate wigs and collars, and jewelry. This is a selection of the most popular symbols.

Wig

Collar ending in falcon heads

Scarab beetle on sacred boat

Red braces

Sun

Winged god with ram's head

Winged Uraeus, the royal cobra

Sokar bird

One of four Sons of Horus

Wedjat eye or Eye of Horus

Nut, the sky goddess

Winged falcon, sacred to the god Horus

Djed pillar

Shen, symbol of eternity

Anubis, god of embalming

Apis bull carrying mummy

Detail from Léon Cogniet's paintings on the ceiling of the Campana room in the Louvre, show one of Napoleon's soldiers transporting a mummy case

Mummy case decoration

There is nothing sad or depressing about Egyptian mummy cases, which are painted in bright and joyful colors. This is because the Egyptians were confident that the dead person had left for a better world. Skilled artists painted the surfaces with beautiful hieroglyphs and religious images. Scenes from the Book of the Dead (pp. 12–13) were common. Other scenes show the sun god, Re, whom the dead person was thought to join in heaven, or the scarab beetle, a symbol of rebirth (p. 44). The various gods associated with Osiris, in particular the four Sons of Horus (p. 20), were also painted on many coffins. Another popular figure was the sky goddess, Nut, who is often seen on the lid or floor of the coffin, with her feathery wings wrapped around the mummy in protection.

SIDE VIEW
Pasenhor was one of the many Libyans who settled in ancient Egypt. This is his outer coffin, made of very thick wood, from about 730 B.C.. The colorful decoration shows up beautifully against the white painted background.

MUMMY BOARD
Mummiform boards were sometimes put on top of the mummy. This board of a priestess from 950–900 B.C. is made of carved wood. This is covered by a layer of plaster painted in raised relief.

Continued on next page

Later mummy cases

By the Late Period of ancient Egyptian history, mummy case production was a thriving industry. Ready-made coffins could be bought off the rack in a range of sizes and styles. Usually an inner, cartonnage case was fitted inside one or two outer cases made of wood. The surface decorations became more and more complicated, and large gods and goddesses were painted on the insides. Designs and hieroglyphs naming and praising the owner were often added, to give each coffin a personal touch.

WHAT'S YOUR SIZE?
The largest outer cases are massive. Under three cases and layers of linen, the person was tiny in comparison.

BIG HEAD, BIG WIG
The outer coffin lid of Nesmin, from about 350 B.C. has a huge head. This is sunk into rounded shoulders carrying a big wig and collar.

Mummy with Ba bird

Hieroglyphs read "all life and power"

SURROUNDED BY GODS
A woman named Seshepenmehit was buried in these two wooden coffins around 650 B.C. The floor of her outer coffin is decorated with a figure of the god Ptah-Sokar-Osiris, a symbol of birth, death, and the afterlife. Both coffin lids are covered in columns of hieroglyphs and scenes from the Book of the Dead (pp. 12–13).

AND ON THE INSIDE...
One of the earliest European pictures of an Egyptian mummy, this engraving was published by a French consul to Egypt in 1735. It shows how the pegs in a wooden mummy case join the lid and base.

Curved lid

Figures of Anubis

Corner posts

LACED FROM BEHIND
Wooden mummy cases came in two parts, the lid and the base. But inner cases made of cartonnage were normally made in one piece. This cartonnage case from c. 850 B.C. would have held the wrapped mummy of a young girl. The mummy must have been placed inside while the linen was damp and flexible. Once the case had dried, its back was laced up like a corset, with thongs that sealed the mummy in. Only then was the case painted.

FOUR-POSTER
Important officials who could not afford a sarcophagus might purchase an extra outer coffin. The priest Hor (c. 680 B.C.) had two mummiform cases, which lay inside a large rectangular box. Also made of wood, this third coffin has a curved lid held up by four corner posts. Every inch of the cases is covered with gods, hieroglyphs, and magic spells.

Cartonnage collar with falcon head at both ends

Apron, a painted body decoration

Face mask

Foot case

REST IN PIECES
The Ptolemaic period began in 323 B.C., when Egypt was conquered by Alexander the Great (p. 29). The inner cases of Ptolemaic mummies consisted of four pieces of cartonnage – the face mask, collar, apron, and foot case. These were placed directly onto the shroud and then held in place with a last layer of bandages.

NOT MASKS
These faces were carved from wood and pegged onto mummy cases.

Ba bird

SACRED BULL
The ancient Egyptians worshiped many animals (pp. 44–47). The sacred Apis Bull was the largest and most important. There was only one Apis at any one time. He was kept in great luxury beside the temple, where he was attended by servants and a harem of cows. This painting on a foot board shows the bull carrying a mummy to its tomb.

UNDER MY TOES
Gilded sandals like these were sometimes painted under a mummy's feet. The figures painted under the mummy's sandals are tiny enemies, symbolizing the dead person's victory over evil.

THE LATEST FASHION, A.D. 200
In the Roman period, from 30 B.C. to A.D. 323, coffins were painted with their owners wearing daily clothes. This Roman woman left for the next world in a bright toga, worn with a stepped wig and a lot of jewelry, including gold rings.

Hieroglyphs

Colorful toga, a long piece of cloth wrapped around the body

Real rings stuck on fingers

Into the sarcophagus

A SARCOPHAGUS IS A COFFIN made of stone. Sarcophagus means "flesh eater" in Greek, for the Greeks believed that the stone would dissolve a dead body. Sarcophagi were expensive, and only pharaohs, noblemen, or important officials were buried in them. They were also incredibly heavy, and had to be positioned in the tomb by gangs of workmen. During the funeral, the mummy was carried into the tomb and sealed in the sarcophagus. The first sarcophagi were plain rectangular boxes, but later ones were rounded to look like the mummies lying inside them.

HEAVY WEIGHT
This huge sarcophagus of basalt is nearly 9 ft (3 m) tall and weighs 4.5 tons. It belonged to Wahibra, an inspector of scribes.

DIGNIFIED IN DEATH
One of the most beautiful royal sarcophagi belongs to Seti I, a great warrior and the father of Ramses the Great (pp. 36, 50–51). His tomb, found in 1817, is cut deep into a cliff in the Valley of the Kings (p. 10). The pharaoh's sarcophagus was in the burial chamber over 330 ft (100 m) below ground. It is made of calcite, a semi-transparent stone. Seti I's mummy, found separately in the royal cache of 1881 (pp. 36–37), was remarkably well-preserved.

VICEROY'S COFFIN
This is the inner sarcophagus of Merymose, the Viceroy of Nubia, c. 1380 B.C. It is one of the first stone coffins made for an important person who was *not* a pharaoh.

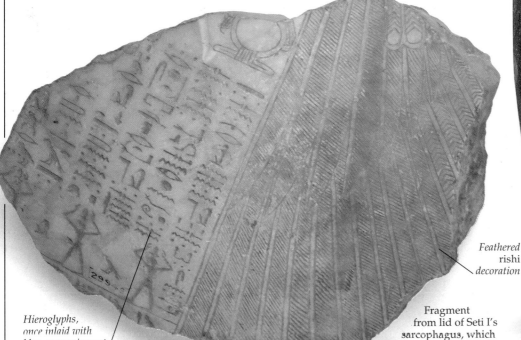

Feathered rishi decoration

Hieroglyphs, once inlaid with blue-green pigment

Fragment from lid of Seti I's sarcophagus, which shattered when lifted

Alexander
the Great

ROYAL BATHTUB
The last Egyptian pharaoh, Nactanebo II, was
buried in this huge sarcophagus. It ended up in
Alexandria, where the Greeks used it as a public
bathtub. Before the hieroglyphics were translated,
it was thought to have belonged to the Greek
ruler Alexander the Great. Alexander's
body has never been found, but ancient
writings claim that he was preserved in a
glass sarcophagus full of honey.

*Drain holes added
for use as bathtub*

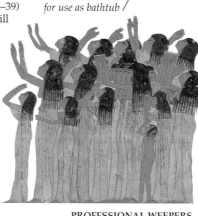

BACK AT REST
Tutankhamun (pp. 38–39)
is the only pharaoh still
lying in his tomb. His
mummy has been
returned to its outer
gilded coffin and
laid back in its huge
sarcophagus. This
stone coffin was
originally housed
inside four gilded
shrines large enough
to drive a car into.
Behind it are wall
paintings showing
sacred funeral rituals.

PROFESSIONAL WEEPERS
Important Egyptians hired mourners for
their funerals. These women would
cry, wail, wave their arms, and
throw dust in the air as the
mummy was dragged into
the tomb and laid in
the sarcophagus.

Howard Carter (far left) watches as
Tutankhamun's outer mummy
case is lifted out
of the sarcophagus

WELL ARMED
This sarcophagus lid,
made of red granite,
covered the mummy of
Setau, the Viceroy of
Nubia. He was buried at
Thebes around 1230 B.C. In
his hands he holds two
magical symbols, the
girdle of Isis (p. 21) and the
djed pillar (pp. 34–35).

HOUSE OF SPIRITS
Like the oldest
mummy cases, early
sarcophagi were
regarded as palaces for
the dead. This rectan-
gular sarcophagus
made of red granite
comes from the Old
Kingdom, around
2500 B.C. At either end
are false doors, for the
mummy's spirit to pass
through when it leaves
and reenters the coffin.

False door

Taking it with you

SLIPPERS, MAKE-UP, A LOAF OF BREAD, a beautiful chair, some favorite earrings – the mummy had to be well prepared to enjoy life in the next world. Most of the artifacts that have survived from ancient Egypt were found in tombs, where they had been buried with the dead. Egypt's warm, dry climate has preserved many objects perfectly. Some mummies took the tools of their trade or symbols of their rank with them to the grave. Tutankhamun (pp. 38–39) was found with his childhood toys. Glamorous women were buried with their wigs, combs, fans, and mirrors. Musicians took along their instruments, and some people were even laid to rest with a board game, to while away the days of leisure in the afterlife.

Corroded bronze surface, once polished for reflection

Make-up compartment

Sliding lid

Sliding lid

Mirror with papyrus decoration on handle

EARTHLY COMFORTS
Sandals were a luxury, as most Egyptians went around barefoot. This padded leather pair is unusual. Most sandals were made from reeds found on the banks of the Nile.

Make-up box in form of stylized lotus flower

Cosmetic spoon in form of lotus flower

Cradle for head

FOREVER BEAUTIFUL
Every mummy wanted to look good for the gods. Ancient Egyptian men, women, and children all wore make-up, particularly *kohl*, a type of eye-paint. *Kohl* looked good and protected against eye infections. Make-up was usually kept in containers decorated with lotus flowers and buds. The lotus, a type of water-lily, was a sacred plant. The Egyptians saw its daily opening and closing as a symbol of life, death, and rebirth.

Lotus stem

Ivory headrest, used instead of a pillow

STAY COOL
In the hot climate, fans were a sign of wealth and sophistication. Pharaohs and other nobles even had special servants just to fan them.

AT YOUR SERVICE
Model servants were placed in the tomb to look after the mummy's every need. This girl is carrying a tray of fresh bread. The walls of tombs were decorated with paintings and sculptures of food, servants, and handy everyday objects. These were thought to come to life inside the sealed tomb.

Brewer

Coffin painting of dead person offering food to gods Re-Harakhty (middle) and Hapy (left), c. 1050 B.C.

DAILY BREAD
Coarse bread was the ancient Egyptians' staple food. Many mummies have badly worn teeth from eating it every day of their lives.

Beer jars

Figs placed in tomb 3,500 years ago

BEER ON TAP
Ancient Egyptians were very fond of beer. By placing a model brewer in their tombs, they hoped to have a steady supply in the afterlife.

Harps were used to play hymns to gods in temple

Pair of bronze cymbals

Ivory feather holder

Wood handle

Ostrich feathers, added according to paintings of fans found on tomb walls

Drawer for holding the pieces

Ivory Senet board

Blue faience game pieces

THE GAME OF LIFE
Senet was ancient Egypt's most popular board game. Senet boards were placed in the tomb to symbolize the dead person's contest with evil to gain eternal life.

ENDLESS JAM
This mummy may have been a professional musician who took his trusty cymbals with him to play in the next world.

Workers for the afterlife

THE ANCIENT EGYPTIANS were an agricultural people, and every year they were all required to do some farming and irrigation work for the government. But rich Egyptians could avoid this work by paying someone to do it for them. When the mummy got to the Field of Reeds, as the Egyptians called heaven, he or she would have to do similar work, sowing and reaping for the god Osiris (pp. 34–35). So from early on, wealthy people were buried with shabtis (worker figures) to do their work after death. Shabtis were inscribed with Chapter Six of the Book of the Dead, which promised "O shabti, if the deceased is called upon to do any of the work required there…you shall say 'Here I am, I will do it.'" In the early New Kingdom (about 1500 B.C.), a single shabti seemed to be enough to guarantee an easy afterlife. But by 1000 B.C., rich Egyptians were being buried with 401 shabtis, one for every day of the year, plus 36 bosses, armed with whips to keep the workers from slacking as they sweated in the heavenly fields.

Overseer or boss shabti wearing skirt and carrying whip

EARLY DIGGER
Before the custom of shabtis, painted wooden servants and workers were placed in tombs. Unlike shabtis, this worker is not shaped like a mummy.

BOX OF WORKERS
Shabti figures were often packed up in beautifully painted wooden boxes. This shabti box belonged to the priestess Henutmehit, whose golden coffins are on page 22.

Dead priestess gives offerings of food to gods

Gilded collar

WOMEN WORKERS
These wooden shabti figures were both made for women from the 18th Dynasty, about 1560 to 1320 B.C.

Nemes *headdress*

Royal cartouche

Shabti of Pharaoh Seti I

Cartouche: oval-shaped inscription with king's name written in hieroglyphs

Shabti of Pharaoh Amenhotep III

Shabti of Pharaoh Amosis

ROYAL SHABTIS
The earliest surviving royal shabti (above) belonged to Amosis, a pharaoh who died in c. 1546. It is wearing a *Nemes* headdress made from cloth folded over the hair. Other royal shabtis, like this one of Amenhotep III (left), wear the domed crown of Upper Egypt.

MODEL COFFINS
Shabtis were sometimes put in elaborate cases made to look like real mummy cases. This one is made of blue faience.

ALL SORTS
Stone, wood, clay, wax, bronze – shabtis were made of all kinds of materials. But the most common was faience, a type of glazed pottery.

WELL EQUIPPED
Many shabtis carry hoes, picks, seed baskets, and other tools. These tell us a lot about farming in ancient Egypt.

Hoe

Pick

Lid of inner wooden case on right

Stone shabti in wooden mummy case and square outer coffin

The mummy and the god Osiris

THE GOD OSIRIS was said to have triumphed over death, and every ancient Egyptian wanted to follow his example. Legend told that far back in history, Osiris was a good pharaoh who was murdered by his evil brother, Seth. But his wife, Isis, and son, Horus, brought Osiris back to life. The story of the dead king's miraculous resurrection gave Egyptians hope in everlasting life. So to be reborn, a dead person tried to be identified with Osiris in every possible way. Mummies were prepared in exactly the same way as the body of Osiris had been long ago. If all went well, the mummy would "become an Osiris" and live forever.

Atef *crown*

Crook

Flail

Brightly colored coffin painting of Osiris wearing cobra crown and protected by falcons

Atef *crown made of two ostrich feathers*

Painted wooden statue of Osiris with green face and *atef* crown

Flail

Crook

TOOLS OF THE TRADE
These two statues of Osiris would have been placed in tombs or temples. They both show Osiris wearing an *atef*, a tall, feathered crown. In his hands the dead pharaoh is holding a crook and a flail. From the earliest times, the Egyptians associated these agricultural tools with kingship and justice. Osiris carried them when he sat and judged dead people's souls in the afterlife (p. 13).

Bronze statue of Osiris wearing *atef* crown

KEEP A STRAIGHT BACK
The djed pillar is an amulet placed in the wrappings of a mummy (pp. 20–21). It was believed to represent the backbone of Osiris, and was thought to give the mummy strength after death.

MUMMY AND SON
The goddess Isis was the wife of Osiris. In this statue she is holding their son, Horus. The ancient Egyptians respected her as a devoted wife and loving mother.

FLAIL
A wooden flail from a statue of Osiris. Like the scepters carried by European kings and queens, the flail was a symbol of power and authority.

GREEN FACE
Among other things, the all-important Osiris was the god of vegetation and natural rebirth. In this role he was connected to the yearly flood of the Nile, which kept Egypt's lands green and fertile. Mummy cases often have green faces to link them with this aspect of Osiris.

Lid with falcon's head

CORN MUMMY
It looks like a real mummy. But inside the linen bandages of this mummy-shaped model are grains of corn, not an embalmed body. The corn "mummy" is wearing a wax mask modeled to look like Osiris. The Egyptians associated the god with the success of the corn harvest. Placed in a tomb, the corn mummy would also help a real mummy to join Osiris in the next world.

Feathered atef *crown*

Wax mask of Osiris

Royal beard

One of four Sons of Horus

Hand holding crook and flail

Djed pillar

GROWING POWER
The power of Osiris was thought to be shown in the sprouting of corn seeds. Figures of the god were even modeled in Nile mud and sown with corn. This one was found in Tutankhamun's tomb (pp. 38–39).

The royal mummies

INSIDE THE PYRAMIDS
The mummies of the kings who built the Giza pyramids have not survived. Despite their hidden entrances sealed with huge blocks of stone, these tombs were looted in ancient times. Once inside, robbers had to find the burial chamber in the darkness, along narrow passages full of false corridors and traps.

THE FAMOUS PHARAOHS of the New Kingdom were buried at Thebes, in a desolate valley called the Valley of the Kings (p. 10). The tombs were cut deep into the rock. But despite all the precautions, they were robbed again and again in ancient times. Each time the priests had to rewrap the mummies and bury them again. Around 1000 B.C., they decided to group the royal mummies together and hide them in two caches (secret hiding places). The dead pharaohs lay hidden in these caches for nearly 3,000 years. The first cache was found in the early 1870s by three brothers who lived nearby. They kept it a secret and began to sell the treasures bit by bit. But the priceless antiquities were eventually traced to them, and in 1881 archae-ologists entered a deep tomb near Deir el-Bahari. They were amazed to find 40 mummies, among them famous pharaohs such as Seti I and Ramses II. The second cache, found in 1898, held another 16 mummies, ten of them royal. When this cache was shipped to Cairo, the customs officers at the city's gate had no idea how to classify it. In the end they decided to tax the dead pharaohs at the same rate as dried fish!

LABELING THE KINGS
To avoid confusion, the priests wrote the pharaohs' names on the outer shrouds. This mummy is inscribed with the name Ramses III.

RAMSES THE GREAT
The famous Ramses II ruled for 67 years, from 1279 to 1212 B.C. He had a reputation as a great warrior, which he seems to have greatly exaggerated. He and his many wives had over 100 children, and he was probably in his nineties when he died. Ancient Egyptians were short by modern standards, around 5 ft 3 in (1.60 m) on average. But Ramses II's mummy, found in the 1881 cache, is 6 ft (1.83 m) tall (p. 50).

REPAIR JOB
The mummy of King Siptah, who died in 1188 B.C., was badly damaged by tomb robbers searching for precious amulets in his bandages. The priests who moved him around 1000 B.C. put his broken arm in a splint before rewrapping him.

Wrapped mummy of King Siptah as it was found in 1881

Unwrapped mummy of King Siptah

GASTON MASPERO
This French archaeologist (third from right) supervised the unwrapping of the royal mummies in Cairo. "And when I see, and touch, the bodies of so many illustrious persons we never imagined could be more than names to us," he wrote later, "I ... find it hard to believe that I am not dreaming."

MISTAKEN IDENTITY

This well-preserved mummy was found wrapped in a shroud inscribed with the name of Tuthmosis I. But examination of the mummy suggests that it is someone else. Surviving historical records show that this pharaoh lived to about 50 years of age. But the mummy is in excellent health and seems to belong to a much younger man. The mummy's true identity is still a mystery.

Nemes headcloth, a sign of royalty

Wood covered in plaster

Remaining fragments of gold leaf

TUTHMOSIS I
A painting in a temple in Thebes shows the real king Tuthmosis I. This accurate copy was made by Howard Carter.

GARLANDS OF FLOWERS
Flower wreaths were placed around a mummy's neck as it was laid in the coffin. When the lid of Amenhotep I's coffin was lifted, the sweet smell of flowers filled the room, 3,000 years after his burial. A wasp that had been attracted by the smell had been trapped in the coffin all those years ago. Its mummified body was found next to the king's.

Ear of corn found in coffin

Fragments of wreaths placed on mummy

UNKNOWN QUEEN

Egyptologists are still not sure about the identity of this elderly woman with wonderful hair. Her mummy was found in the second royal cache of 1898. Some experts believe she is Hatshepsut, a female pharaoh who is often shown wearing the royal false beard. Others think she is Queen Tiy, one of the wives of Amenhotep III. Tiy is probably the grandmother of Tutankhamun (pp. 38–39).

ROYAL COFFIN
The mummy case of King Intef (c. 1650 B.C.) is made from a hollowed-out tree trunk. This was plastered and covered with gold leaf engraved with a *rishi* feather design (p. 23). Robbers often stripped the gold leaf off royal coffins like this.

A KING AT REST
The second cache of royal mummies was found in the tomb of Amenhotep II in 1898. Most of the mummies were shipped to Cairo, but Amenhotep was left lying in his sarcophagus where he had been found. Shortly after this photo was taken, a band of robbers overcame the armed guards and ripped open his bandages, looking for valuable amulets.

CRUEL DEATH
The strangest body found among the royal mummies was this unknown man. His face is distorted with agony, and his mouth is open as if he was screaming. He must have died horribly, perhaps by being poisoned, suffocated, or even buried alive. His body was wrapped in a sheepskin, a material the Egyptians thought was unclean. No one knows what horrible crime he committed to deserve such a cruel death.

The treasures of Tutankhamun

Howard Carter (center) and his team stare in wonder at the sarcophagus through a door in the fourth shrine

On NOVEMBER 26, 1922, Howard Carter peered through a small hole into a dark tomb in the Valley of the Kings (pp. 10, 36–37)." As my eyes grew accustomed to the light," he wrote later, "… I was struck dumb with amazement." The English archaeologist and his rich supporter, Lord Carnarvon, had just discovered the tomb of the pharaoh Tutankhamun, sealed over 3,200 years before. Five years of exploration had led them to the only fully intact royal tomb ever found – and probably the most exciting archaeological discovery ever made. Inside was the king's mummy, wearing a superbly crafted mask of solid gold. The body lay in a nest of three gold mummy cases, each fitting inside the next. The cases rested in turn in a sarcophagus surrounded by four gilded wooden shrines and an amazing array of statues, furniture, and jewelry. As Carter put it, it was a room full of "gold – everywhere the glint of gold."

KING AND QUEEN
The carving on this ebony and ivory box shows Tutankhamun in a garden receiving flowers from his queen. When his father, the powerful pharaoh Akhenaten, died, Tutankhamun was no more than nine years old. He probably never had much real power, and would barely be remembered if his tomb had not survived in such perfect condition.

SCARAB PENDANT
This pendant of a winged scarab beetle is made of gold and semi-precious stones. The design spells out the three hieroglyphs – Neb, Kheperu, and Re – of Tutankhamun's name.

Gold sheets covering wood frame

Small shrine made to hold a sacred statue

Decorated panels

Silver door bolts

Sled runners so shrine could be dragged into tomb

THE KING'S DUMMY
This painted wooden "dummy" shows the king as he must have looked when he died c. 1324 B.C. It was probably dressed in his clothes and jewelry.

Shaved head

Bead vest

THE MUMMY
The king's mummy was poorly preserved because of chemical reactions with embalming resins. He was slightly built and stood about 5 ft 5 in (1.65 m) tall. Studies of his teeth gave an age of 16 or 17, though he may have been as old as 22. X-rays showed damage to his skull, but his actual cause of death is uncertain. The uneasy political situation during his reign suggests that he may have been murdered.

Hunting scene

Nemes *headdress, a symbol of royalty*

Syrians   Tutankhamun   Fan bearers   King's soldiers
in his chariot

PAINTED BOX
This wooden box was stuffed with clothes, including
the pharaoh's sandals. It is painted with scenes from
Tutankhamun's life. On this side, he can be seen leading his
army to victory over the Syrians. But it is unlikely that the
king ever went to war, and the painting is thought to be a
symbolic representation of the pharaoh's supreme power.
In two similar scenes on the lid, the young king hunts lions,
ostriches, and antelopes in the desert.

Falcon-headed
collar

SLOW GOING
An Italian newspaper from
1924 tells the tale of the
amazing discovery. Though
Carter and Carnavon found
the tomb in November
1922, Carter was so careful
and painstaking in his work
that he didn't begin to open
the coffins until October
1925. It took him almost a
decade to examine the
entire contents of the tomb.

GOLD MASK
The king's mummy mask was made of solid gold inlaid with
colorful glass and stones, including dark blue lapis lazuli. It
weighed over 22.5 lb (10.2 kg). The pharaoh is wearing a *nemes*
headdress (p. 33), and a vulture and a cobra sit on his brow.

Inlaid lapis
lazuli, a
blue stone

A NEST OF GOLD AND GEMSTONES
This is Tutankhamun's middle mummy case. Like the outer case, it
was made of wood covered in gold and colored stones. It fitted so
snugly inside the outer case that Carter had a lot of difficulty lifting
it out. Inside it was a third, inner case. This was solid
gold and weighed an unbelievable 245 lb (110.4 kg).

Inlaid pieces of red, blue,   Feathered *rishi design*
and turquoise glass

Curse of the mummy

"DEATH SHALL COME ON SWIFT WINGS to him that toucheth the tomb of pharaoh." In the spring of 1923, newspapers around the world claimed that this dramatic inscription had been found inside Tutankhamun's tomb (pp. 38–39). The excitement was caused by the sudden death of Lord Carnarvon, one of the first to enter the tomb. Many people claimed that the dead pharaoh was angry and had "cursed" all those who had disturbed his rest. The curse has since been blamed for the deaths of many people connected with the discovery. Some now believe that the deaths may have been caused by bacteria or even atomic radiation sealed inside the tomb. But the deaths can all be explained, and the famous inscription never existed. Howard Carter and most of the others who entered the tomb lived on for many years. The most important wish of a pharaoh was that his name should live forever. Considering how famous Tutankhamun has become since his tomb was found, he should be pleased, not angry.

MUMMY POWDERS
Ground-up mummy was believed to have magical powers. It was used as an occult potion, and was a popular medicine in the 16th and 17th centuries. Powdered mummy was also used to make brown pigment for artists. The paint was called *Caput Mortuum*, Latin for "dead head."

FIRST VICTIM
Lord Carnarvon, Howard Carter's sponsor, had first come to Egypt because of his poor health. Early in 1923, he was bitten by a mosquito, and the bite became infected after he reopened it while shaving. A fever developed, and he died on April 5, 1923, just over four months after he and Carter had entered Tutankhamun's tomb. It was later said that the lights of Cairo went out at the moment of his death. Another story associated with the curse was that Carter's canary had been swallowed by a cobra on the day the tomb was opened. Tutankhamun's famous mummy mask has a cobra on the brow.

Lord Carnarvon's death certificate

Lord Carnarvon's cutthroat razor

Real mummy of Ramses III

DANGEROUS SPELLS
This is one of four "magic bricks" that were found in the tomb of the priestess Henutmehit (pp. 22, 32). The bricks were placed at the four corners of the tomb and were believed to have supernatural powers. A spell from the Book of the Dead was inscribed on the mud surface of each brick. One of them reads "You who come to trap (steal), I will not let you trap … I am the protection for the Osiris Henutmehit." This was meant to keep away any intruders who might disturb the priestess' mummy in her tomb.

Wooden figure attached to magic brick

Inscription in hieratic, a script that developed from hieroglyphics

Clay brick

Boris Karloff in *The Mummy*

THE MUMMY BECOMES A FILM STAR
The angry mummy disturbed from the sleep of centuries proved a great subject for horror films. The first was *The Mummy*, from 1932, which starred Boris Karloff as the mummified priest Imhotep (above). His appearance was based on the real mummy of the pharaoh Ramses III (left), found in the 1881 royal cache (pp. 36–37). In the film, Imhotep is brought back to life by a magic spell read aloud by an archaeologist.

THE MUMMY'S REVENGE
Alongside *Dracula* and *Frankenstein*, the mummy bent on revenge became one of the most popular monsters in Hollywood horror films. This is a poster for a 1959 remake of *The Mummy*, made in color and starring Christopher Lee. The many other films included *The Mummy's Hand*, *The Mummy's Shroud*, *The Mummy's Curse*, *Blood from the Mummy's Tomb* – even *Abbott and Costello Meet the Mummy*.

The archaeologist's assistant in *Raiders of the Lost Ark* finds herself face to face with a tomb full of mummies

LOST IN THE TOMB
A newspaper story from 1934 tells of a Hungarian tourist who was lost in the tomb of Ramses II during a visit to the Valley of the Kings. She was found the next day, lying speechless at the foot of a statue of the pharaoh. Passing a night in the cold, pitch-black tomb had completely terrified her.

SILENT SHRIEK
Many mummy heads were collected in the 19th century and displayed as curiosities in European homes. Travelers to Egypt could buy them from dealers as part of a busy souvenir trade. This gruesome head was mounted under a glass dome. Nobody knows where it comes from, whom it belonged to, or how old it is. Its grizzly features inspired some of the mummies used as props in the popular 1981 film *Raiders of the Lost Ark*. These were made of silicon rubber.

Greek and Roman mummies

MANY GREEKS HAD SETTLED IN EGYPT long before it was invaded by Alexander the Great (p. 29) in 323 B.C. Like the Romans who arrived in 30 B.C., the Greeks adopted the Egyptian custom of mummification. They took great care in wrapping their dead in elaborate geometric patterns. But beneath the linen, Greek and Roman mummies are usually badly embalmed. The mummies were laid to rest in open ground, not tombs, and several generations were often buried together in family graves. Some of the most interesting mummies from the Roman period were discovered in a cemetery in the Faiyum region of Egypt. Instead of having idealized faces like the ones found on Egyptian masks, they wear a realistic picture of the dead person. This sometimes takes the form of a plaster mask. But more often, portraits were painted on a wooden panel or straight onto the shroud.

ROMAN CAT
The ancient Greeks and Romans made mummies of all kinds of animals (pp. 44–47). This preserved cat is wearing a painted plaster mask. Two colors of linen bandages have been wrapped in an intricate "window" pattern.

THE LIVING DEAD
These mummy portraits are painted on wooden panels in colored wax. They may have been done while the person was alive and hung in the home until he or she died. The hairstyles, jewelry, and clothing tell us a lot about everyday life in Roman-occupied Egypt around the time of Christ.

Gilded studs

FOREVER YOUNG
X-rays of this mummy of a Roman boy showed that he was in his early teens when he died. The elaborate bandages are decorated with gilded studs.

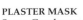

PLASTER MASK
Some Greek mummies wore plaster masks that made them look like they were sitting up in the coffin. Many of these masks are covered in gold and have inset eyes of stone or glass to make them look more realistic.

Painted foot case

GOLDEN GIRL
This Roman girl died in Egypt at the age of eight or nine. She was not properly embalmed, but her skin was coated in a dark, liquid resin to make it tough and waterproof. Her body was then covered in thin pieces of beaten gold. These were meant to connect her to the sun god, who was thought to have flesh of gold.

Inscription in Greek

Gold eye covers

Gold tongue cover

Gold nipple covers

Figure of Osiris

MUMMY I.D.
Mixing up the bodies in the embalming tent could have been disastrous. To avoid confusion, Roman embalmers tied a wooden label around each mummy's neck. Mummy labels are often inscribed with the dead person's name, his or her age, profession, parents, even the date of death or where the mummy was to be buried. Some labels also carry a prayer for the dead person's soul, which relatives had bought instead of a tombstone.

GOLD LEAVES
The Romans placed pieces of gold over a mummy's sensitive parts. The tongue plate was probably meant to allow the mummy to speak.

Side view of Roman girl's head, showing eyelashes and gold leaf on face

Pieces of gold leaf

ROYAL BIRD
The falcon soared to great heights in the skies of ancient Egypt. So it is not surprising that it became associated with the sky god, Horus, who came to life as the pharaoh. In Greek and Roman times, falcons were mummified by the thousands and buried in special cemeteries with other sacred animals (pp. 44–47).

DEATH OF CLEOPATRA
Cleopatra, the last Greek ruler of Egypt, died in 30 B.C. Roman historians said that she committed suicide by holding a poisonous snake to her breast. Though there is no evidence to support the story, it has been painted and retold many times. Cleopatra's body was probably mummified and buried with all the ceremony due to an Egyptian queen. She was supposedly buried lying next to her lover, Mark Antony, but their tomb has never been found.

Animal mummies

THE ANCIENT EGYPTIANS MUMMIFIED many animals with the same care they took for people. Favorite pets were occasionally mummified and put in the tomb with their owners to keep them company in the afterlife. But most animals were embalmed for religious reasons. Animals were thought to be representatives or spiritual messengers of the gods. Many gods became naturally associated with one or more animals that shared the same qualities. The cow, for instance, which took such tender care of its young, was associated with Hathor, the goddess of love and motherhood. Special places became the centers of worship for major gods and goddesses. Here the animals sacred to these gods were mummified and buried in enormous cemeteries. By the later period of ancient Egyptian history, a huge religious industry flourished and millions of animals were bred just to be mummified.

SACRED BULL
When he died, the sacred Apis Bull (p. 27) was embalmed with the same care and ceremony shown to a pharaoh.

Mummy of a wild dog or jackal, sacred to Anubis, the god of embalming (pp. 10, 13–15).

Bronze case for the mummy of a shrew mouse, sacred animal of the god Horus (p. 20)

ROYAL SERPENT
Bronze container for the mummy of an eel or cobra. The snake's beard and crown show its association with royalty.

A limestone case for a mummified scarab beetle, the smallest creature to be embalmed

ROLLING ACROSS THE SKY
The scarab beetle rolls up balls of dung and pushes them around. The Egyptians believed the beetle god Khepri rolled the sun across the sky in the same way.

TWINS
These two falcons were embalmed and mummified together, to strengthen their magical association with the god Horus (p. 20).

Unwrapped mummy of a crocodile

Reeds used to pad out crocodile shape

Linen bandages

ON THE MENU?
An unwrapped mummified fish. Fish were sacred in some parts of Egypt, where they were never caught or eaten. In other areas, they were on the menu. This often led to violent conflicts between neighboring towns.

IN THE NILE, CROCODILE
In ancient times, the Nile River was full of crocodiles, which were feared for their ferocity. They were sacred to Sobek, a god of the water. Tame crocs were kept in luxury, fed on fine meats and wine and dressed in gold jewelry. The largest mummified crocodile ever found was 15 ft (4.6 m) long.

Painted plaster mask for a falcon mummy

Head of a mummified goose, sacred to the god Amun

SACRED IBIS
Three kinds of ibis were found in ancient Egypt. The migrant species with brown plumage still visits the country every year. But the bronze-colored crested ibis and the beautiful sacred ibis (right) are now extinct there.

Head and neck made of bronze

SCRIBE GOD
This gold container holds the mummified body of an ibis. Four million embalmed ibises were discovered at a single animal cemetery, each in its individual pot. They would have been dedicated to Thoth, the god of scribes and writing. Thoth was usually depicted with a human body and the head of an ibis.

Wooden body covered in gold leaf

Feet made of bronze

ROOST IN PEACE
The mummy of a falcon lies in this coffin made of cartonnage (p. 18). The lid is richly painted with a floral collar and a winged scarab beetle. The designs are just like the ones on human mummy cases.

Prominent teeth

Geometric wrapping common in Roman period

Eyes, which bulge on top of crocodile's head

Continued on next page

Continued from previous page

The sacred cat

The graceful, green-eyed cats that leaped and purred around ancient Egyptian homes were a lot like the pets we keep today. Ancient Egyptian records show that cats were kept as pets as early as 2100 B.C. By the late period of ancient Egyptian history, the cat was a sacred animal. Writing about 450 B.C., the Greek historian Herodotus (p. 14) described how carefully cats were protected. Anyone who killed a cat could be punished by death. When a cat died, some families even took their beloved pet's body to the city of Bubastis, the center of worship for the cat goddess Bastet. Here the dead pet was embalmed, wrapped, and laid in a special cat-shaped coffin before being buried in a cat cemetery.

CAT WRAP
To mummify a cat, the embalmers began by removing its insides. Then they filled the pet's body cavity with earth or sand and wrapped it in bandages that had been soaked in natron (pp. 14-15) or treated with resin. This fine mummy is wrapped in an elaborate diamond pattern.

Green head symbolizes bronze mask worn by mummy

White body represents linen wrappings of mummy inside case

Mummified cat

Cat mummy with comical face

TIGHT FIT
To produce a compact mummy, the embalmers laid the cat's front legs by its side and tucked its back legs up against its belly. The cat's tail was then curled up between its feet.

46

Pierced ear, which probably once held a gold earring

BRONZE BASTET
The yearly festival celebrating the cat goddess Bastet was one of the most important events on the ancient Egyptian calendar. This statue of Bastet made from bronze has inlaid eyes of colored glass. Many of these elegant figures wore gold rings in their ears and noses. Thousands of images of Bastet were set up in temples by priests, so worshipers could place offerings of food and milk before them. The priests also bred many cats specially for mummification.

Bronze container made to hold the mummified paw of a cat

THE BALD TRUTH
Shaving was seen as a way of cleansing the spirit, and ancient Egyptian priests and priestesses all shaved their heads. When a pet cat died, a whole household might go into mourning and shave their eyebrows as a mark of respect.

Wooden case with door at back

PURR-SONALIZED COFFINS
These wooden cat coffins were all found at Bubastis, the biggest center of cat worship. Each one contained the well-wrapped mummy of a cat. The largest one shows an idealized, graceful cat, but the other two are more natural and humorous. In the 19th century, some 300,000 Egyptian cat mummies were shipped to Liverpool in England, where they were turned into fertilizer and sold by the ton.

Unwrapping the mummy's secrets

THE SCIENTIFIC STUDY OF MUMMIES does more than reveal how the ancient Egyptians embalmed their dead. Autopsies of ancient bodies can also show how people lived, what they ate, and what diseases they suffered from. In the 19th century, many mummies were unwrapped by surgeons. But their findings were limited by the technology of the age. Nowadays ruining the careful bandaging and dissecting the body is considered destructive and disrespectful. The invention of X-ray analysis in 1895 meant that mummies could be electronically "unwrapped" without being damaged. Early equipment was heavy and awkward. But by the 1960s, powerful, mobile X-ray units that could be brought into museums had been developed. The latest scanning equipment can "see" through the bandages and create complex, three-dimensional images of the body within. A small tissue sample from the mummy can be rehydrated (made wet again) and its cell structure studied. Even DNA, a person's basic genetic structure, can be identified. Some scientists believe that genetic analysis of mummies may one day help find a cure for modern viruses.

CAIRO AUTOPSY
Daniel Fouquet, a French doctor, unwraps the mummy of Tawedjatra, a priestess who died around 1000 B.C. This historic autopsy took place at the Cairo Museum in 1891. It was attended by the leading French Egyptologists of the day, along with several society women.

ESTIMATING AGE
This mummy of a man is lying in a coffin made c. 1000 B.C. for Tawuhenut, a female singer. Studies of the man's teeth and bones put his age at 20 to 35. More accurate estimates can be made for mummies who died before the age of 25 when their teeth and bones were still growing.

UNDER THE MICROSCOPE
In 1908, Dr. Margaret Murray (second from right) and her colleagues unwrapped and dissected a mummy at Manchester University in England. They kept some tissue samples. These were examined in the 1970s as part of a major mummy survey led by Dr. Rosalie David. When rehydrated and viewed under a microscope, the tissues revealed evidence of a lung disease called silicosis. Desert sandstorms and the dusty climate may have caused breathing problems like silicosis for many ancient Egyptians.

Artificial eyes

Scarab beetle amulet with wings wrapping around neck

Dense mass may be a pot

ALL IS REVEALED
This is a xeroradiograph (a special high-definition X-ray) of a mummy wrapped around 1000 B.C. Unlike normal X-rays, xeroradiographs emphasize edges, so that outlines of shapes are easier to see. This makes it easier to locate amulets (pp. 20–21), wrapped organs, and bones. This image revealed a lot of packing material which was pushed under the skin to make the shrunken body appear more lifelike.

Arms by sides (not crossed over) with hands covering genitals

Edge of linen bandages

Atef crown of two feathers, a symbol of the god Osiris

Holes in skull

Badly bent bones

BONE DISEASE
This cartonnage coffin from the 22nd Dynasty (945–715 B.C.) once held the mummy of a child. All that remains of the body is a skeleton. Medical experts found that the strange deformities in the skull and other bones were caused by a rare bone disease called osteogenesis imperfecta. This would have afflicted the child while still in the mother's womb. He or she must have been born with brittle bones and probably died soon after.

Facial features painted on wrappings

Ear wrapped separately

MALE DANCER
This unusual mummy from Egypt's Roman period (pp. 42–43) was found lying in the coffin of a woman dating from much earlier. From the packing, which emphasizes the shapes of the breasts and thighs, it was assumed that the mummy was female. But X-rays taken in the 1960s revealed a man's body beneath the wrappings. The paintings on the linen represent body tattoos. He may have been a dancer who performed at religious ceremonies and banquets, because such dancers are known to have had similar tattoos. The embalmers wrapped the mummy with great care, packing it to give it the shape of a living body. The facial features were painted on, in the style of Old Kingdom mummies. The fingers and toes are all wrapped separately, even in the outer layers. This is very rare.

Elaborate geometric wrapping on forearms, typical of Roman period

Side view of Roman mummy, showing careful wrapping of individual fingers

Tattoo painted onto wrappings

Piece of jewelry inset in sandal

MUMMY FINGERPRINT
Even after 3,000 years, it is still possible to take a mummy's fingerprints. Police forensic experts at Scotland Yard in London, England, have the prints of an Egyptian mummy in their records of modern criminals. They took the prints from a mummy's hand lent to them by the British Museum.

Linen sandals

Continued on next page

ROYAL VISIT TO PARIS

In 1974, experts in Egypt discovered that Ramses II's skin was being destroyed by a mysterious infection. The royal mummy was flown to Paris three years later for medical treatment. International regulations required him to have a passport, which gave his occupation as "King (deceased)." When he arrived in France, a team of conservators successfully cured the infection, which turned out to be a fungus. A total of 102 specialists, including radiographers, police forensic scientists, botanists, and textile experts, examined the ancient pharaoh's body.

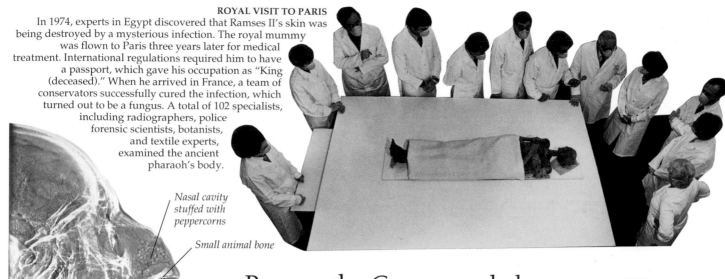

Nasal cavity stuffed with peppercorns

Small animal bone

Missing teeth

STUCK UP

This xeroradiograph (p. 49) revealed the secret of the mummy's dignified profile. The embalmers had kept the king's nose in the air by packing it with peppercorns and propping it with a tiny animal bone.

Ramses the Great revealed

The mummy of Ramses II was found in 1881 (p. 36) and has been resting in the Cairo Museum ever since. A special trip to Paris in 1977 gave medical experts from around the world a unique chance to examine the dead pharaoh's body. It is interesting to compare their findings with the historical records of his 67-year reign. X-rays showed a battle wound on one shoulder and signs of a healed fracture in one toe. The king may have suffered these injuries in an accident in the desert, an event described in ancient records. Close examination revealed a tiny piece of blue and gold fabric stuck to the mummy's skin. This was probably part of the king's clothes. Traces of unusual sand suggest that he may have been embalmed near Per-Ramesse, the king's northern capital. Analysis of resins identified the herbs and flowers used to embalm him. Ramses's body was especially rich in camomile oil. It was also coated with an extract from a wild tobacco plant, possibly added to keep insects off the body.

THE LIVING PHARAOH

This is Ramses II as he may have looked in life. Painted by Winifred Brunton in 1920, it was based on a comparison of his mummy and ancient sculptures. There is a striking physical resemblance between Ramses II, his father, Seti I (p. 28), and his son, Merenptah. The mummies of the three kings all have large, hooked noses.

REDHEAD

Considering he is more than 3,260 years old, Ramses II is in very good health. His hair was probably dyed with henna but seems to have been naturally red. His slightly open mouth reveals a good set of teeth. Abscesses in his jaw must have caused him great pain. The king also suffered from blood circulation problems and severe arthritis in the hips. This must have made it hard for him to get around in his last years. He was probably in his nineties when he died and had a bent back. To keep his head up, the embalmers had to break his spine.

CAT scanning

Since 1977, doctors have been examining mummies with the help of an advanced X-ray process called CAT scanning. CAT stands for computerized axial tomography (the last word means "cut" or "section"). A normal X-ray produces one flat view of an object. But a CAT scan takes many thin views, each one like a slice of bread. These are then processed by a computer and put together to produce the whole loaf – a three-dimensional image of the object and all its surfaces, inside and out. It is possible to zoom in on one slice or isolate a particular part of the mummy to study it in more detail. The thickness of the slices can also be varied to give more information on one area like the skull or teeth. In 1991, doctors at St. Thomas's Hospital in London, England, began a mummy scanning program with the British Museum. The first mummy they studied was Tjentmutengebtiu, a priestess who died around 900 B.C. She is enclosed in a beautiful cartonnage case that would be damaged if it were opened.

Cartonnage mummy case of Tjentmutengebtiu

Edge of mummy mask

Artificial eyes

Winged amulet

Metal hawk-shaped amulet

Metal embalming plate

Metal amulet over genitals

Outline of mummy case

Winged metal amulet lying on feet

Mummy wrappings

Skeleton of mummy

TV CELEBRITY
Radiographers view the scanning process on high resolution television screens in a separate observation booth. They can control the thickness of the individual slices. The radiographers took slices 0.1 in (2 mm) thick of Tjentmutengebtiu's head and neck and 0.2 in (4 mm) thick for the rest of her body. It took a total of over 500 slices to scan the mummy from head to toe.

X-RAY VIEWING
The CAT scanner can also simulate normal, flat X-ray images (above). Dense structures like bones are shown in white. Less dense materials like bandages come out dark blue or black. These X-rays show the skeleton inside the mummy and the mummy lying inside its case. The mummy mask, artificial eyes, various amulets, and an embalming plate can also be seen.

Dr. Stephen Hughes (left) and Dr. Ajit Sofat prepare the mummy of Tjentmutengebtiu to be CAT scanned

COMPUTER GRAPHICS
CAT scans tell doctors a lot about the density of objects hidden beneath the surface. Different tissues like bone or skin have their own distinctive densities. Once these have been calculated, one tissue can be isolated from the others. This is the skin on Tjentmutengebtiu's skull. The doctors can even look inside her skull and see details like the sinus cavities. Information on density can also reveal if an object like an amulet is made of clay or metal.

Mummies of the Andes

Dancing demon figure from Paracas, Peru, where many mummy bundles were found

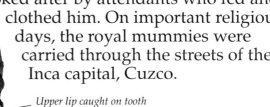

Helmet

Mace

Shield

POTTERY WARRIOR
The Moche were a farming and fishing people who lived on the northern coast of Peru from 200 B.C. to about A.D. 600. They made beautiful pottery to bury with their dead.

THE EARLIEST MUMMIES FROM THE ANDES region of South America were made by fishing people who lived along the coasts of Chile and Peru. By 3000 B.C., they were preserving their dead by drying them in the sun and sometimes removing their internal organs, too. Mummies from various later cultures have been found all over modern Colombia, Ecuador, Peru, and Chile, from the high mountain peaks to the dry coastal lowlands. Many of these cultures treated the mummies of their ancestors as sacred objects. The Incas, who ruled most of the Andes region when the Europeans arrived in A.D. 1532, believed their dead king was a god. By worshiping his mummy, they hoped to keep his soul alive. A dead king's mummy was seated on a throne and looked after by attendants who fed and clothed him. On important religious days, the royal mummies were carried through the streets of the Inca capital, Cuzco.

WILD CAT GOD
Cloth was highly valued by the ancient Peruvians. They were great weavers and embroiderers who regarded cloth as a form of wealth. This tapestry of a cat god was woven by the Chancay people (A.D. 1000–1470). The Chancay did not have pet cats, so it must represent a wild cat like the puma or jaguar. Great quantities of colorful fabric were sealed inside tombs. Mummies were also wrapped in many layers of cloth specially made for the purpose. Fine-quality garments were believed to show a person's importance. Weavers must have spent several years making the fabric for the most splendid mummies. Some burials even included cloth-making tools like looms, spindles, and thread.

Upper lip caught on tooth

Rope used to bundle body up

Well-preserved toenails

UNWRAPPED PERUVIAN MUMMY
Some Peruvian mummies were carefully embalmed. This involved removing the internal organs, smoke-drying the body, and rubbing it with oils, resins, and herbs. But most mummies were preserved by natural conditions – either the hot dry climate of the coast or the freezing cold of the Andes Mountains. The drying process was probably helped by the layers of fabric, which helped draw off the body fluids. The dead person was usually placed in a sitting position with the knees drawn up against the chest. The hands were flattened over the face, and the arms and legs were bound tightly in place.

DESERT CEMETERY
The dry climate of the Peruvian coast was ideal for drying out mummies. In the 1880s, several hundred well-preserved mummies were found among the thousands of graves in the vast desert cemetery at Ancón. The high levels of natural salts in the soil seem to have helped preserve the bodies, including the mummies of pet dogs.

Male figure Female figure

FERTILITY OFFERINGS
The Chancay people placed pottery with their dead. These hollow figures of a man and a woman stood on either side of a mummy. They were probably once wrapped in bright textiles.

FALSE HEAD
This is a false head worn by one of the mummies found at Ancón, Peru, in the 1880s. It is like a cushion made of painted cotton stuffed with leaves or seaweed. The nose and mouth are carved wood. The eyes are shells, with small drops of resin for pupils. The hair is made of plant fiber dyed black. This is wrapped in a headband and crowned with a headdress made of brilliant green parrot feathers. In ancient Peru, such headdresses were a sign of high status.

Striped mantle (cloak)

Belt from which pouches hang

HIGH IN THE ANDES
A side view shows the pouches that hang from a belt around the mummy's middle. They contain avocado seeds, raw cotton, and coca leaves, which the Chimu chewed to relax. These leaves contain the drug cocaine.

False head

Copper eyes

Copper nose and mouth

Feather eyelashes

MUMMY BUNDLE
The Chimu were a highly developed farming people from northern Peru. Their kingdom flourished from A.D. 1000 until 1470, when they were conquered by the Incas. This is a Chimu mummy bundle with a false head. It contains a crouching body wrapped in many layers of fine cotton and wool cloth. X-rays revealed that the dead person's eyes were covered by plates of metal, probably gold. A bracelet was also seen on one wrist, and shells had been placed at the mummy's heels.

Pouch

53

Continued on next page

Continued from previous page

False head

Wig of long strands of human hair

Leaf packing

Animal skin

Mantle

PARACAS NECKLACE
This cloth necklace was found in the desolate Paracas Peninsula, on Peru's south coast. Hundreds of mummies dating from 1000 to 200 B.C. have been found in ancient cemeteries there.

Tiny human figures

SACRED DOLL
Found in the Pacasmayo Valley in Peru, this doll is made from woven tapestry, cloth, and reeds. She is holding a bundle of raw cotton. Cotton was one of the first crops to be grown in the Andes, and evidence of it goes back to 3000 B.C. The doll may be a goddess buried with a dead person to bring him or her luck.

INSIDE THE BUNDLE
This cross-section of a mummy bundle was drawn during the excavations of Ancón, Peru, in the 1880s. The mummy was found with a few vases in a grave about 10 ft (3 m) deep. Its false head includes a wig of human hair. Beneath the layers of colorful cloth, the dried body had been wrapped in an animal skin and tied up tightly.

Feathered headdress

Plaited hair band

SNAKE EMBROIDERY
The Paracas Peninsula is famous for its ancient textiles, found either with or as part of mummy bundles. Some bundles contained over 100 cotton garments. Shirts, mantles (cloaks), ponchos, skirts, loincloths, and turbans have all been found. Many of them are embroidered in wool with birds, animals, fish, and imaginary beasts.

Silver plate held between teeth

Cotton wrapping

Matting of raffia, a kind of palm

Stirrup spout

Turban

Feathered vest

Ear spools

MOCHE STIRRUP POT
The Moche made fine pottery vessels and figures to put in tombs. They even used clay molds to mass-produce favorite designs. The pots often have spouts shaped like stirrups. The head of a Moche lord forms the body of this pot. His earlobes are stretched and he wears the large ear spools worn by important Moche men.

Pair of gold ear spools

BUNDLED UP
The Chancay culture flourished on the central coast of Peru from c. 1000 to 1470. When ordinary Chancas died, they were wrapped in plain cloth and buried in simple pits with a few goods. But the rich were buried in great tombs, some with stairs leading down to them. These contained many rooms full of beautiful gifts. This Chanca woman was probably wrapped in palm matting. She is wearing clothes of cotton and feathers. Her mouth was packed with llama wool and sealed with a silver plate.

Sandals made of raffia fiber

SILENT SCREAM

Mexican museums contain many ancient mummies like this one. More recent preserved bodies have become tourist attractions. The gruesome mummies on display in Wanna Watto, a vast cemetery in Mexico City, are all from this century.

Sewn-up eyes

Sewn-up mouth

Plaited hair

SHRUNKEN HEAD

The Jivaro Indians of the Amazon were among the many groups of people who used to shrink their enemies' heads. They believed a person's soul lived in the head. By owning an enemy's head, a Jivaro warrior could possess some of the dead person's spiritual strength. The Jivaro shrunk the heads to less than half their original size in an elaborate process that lasted six days. They then decorated the hair, which did not shrink, with beads and feathers. The result was a *tsantsa*, or trophy head. Warriors wore *tsantsas* around their necks at special festivals.

Other American mummies

Mummies have been found in many parts of the American continent, from Argentina in the south to as far north as Alaska. Some of the earliest bodies, from the first century B.C., come from the Kentucky region. Most of these mummies have been found in caves, like the bodies of Navahos in Arizona. The freezing cold has preserved the tattooed bodies of Inuit in Alaska. The inhabitants of the nearby Aleutian Islands buried their dead in warm volcanic caves, which helped to dry them out. Some of the bodies found here were stuffed with dry grass after the insides were removed. In South America, mummies have been found in many places beyond Peru. The Jivaro Indians of the Amazon even shrunk the severed heads of their enemies.

CHILEAN GIRL

At its height, the empire of the Incas stretched from Ecuador in the north to Bolivia and Chile in the south. This is the freeze-dried mummy of an Incan girl found high in the Andes in Chile. The Incas practiced human sacrifice. During droughts or other times of crisis, children were sometimes selected, with their parents' approval, to be mummified and offered to the gods. When a king died, some of his favorite wives and servants were killed. They were then mummified so they could accompany the dead king on his journey to the next world.

COLOMBIAN MUMMY

This mummy of a woman was found with 13 others in a cave near Bogotá, in the Colombian Andes. She is wearing a necklace of animal teeth and pieces of carved sea shell. Her internal organs were removed through an incision at the base of the spine. Her hands were then tied across her chest, after which her body may have been smoke-dried.

Mark of tightly wrapped cloth on skin

Badly worn teeth

Dry, papery skin

The Iceman

ONE AUTUMN DAY OVER 5,300 YEARS AGO, an exhausted traveler was surprised by a sudden snowstorm high in the Alps. He took shelter in a gully between two ridges of rock. But the storm was fierce, and he died from exposure and cold where he lay. Snow covered his body, and he was soon frozen into a glacier. Winters came and went, centuries passed, the empires of Egypt, Greece, and Rome rose and fell. Europe was ravaged by two world wars, but still the dead man lay frozen in time, until freak weather in the summer of 1991 exposed his body once again. After it had been found, a technique called radiocarbon dating was used to estimate the body's age. It showed that the Iceman, as he is now known, died between 3350 and 3300 B.C. This makes him the oldest well-preserved mummy in the world. More than 70 objects were found with him. They are not grave goods, but personal possessions he was carrying when he died. Teams of specialists are now studying the Iceman's body, clothing, tools, and weapons. Botanists are examining the plant matter found on his body, which may show where he was from. His blood, bones, vital organs, and DNA may reveal the diseases he suffered from. All of this research may give clues to who the Iceman was, and how he lived and died.

THE DISCOVERY
On September 19, 1991, two German climbers found a body frozen in the top of a glacier. It was about 10,000 ft (3,000 m) up in a remote part of the Alps near the Austrian-Italian border. The body had been partly uncovered because of a freak storm in the Sahara Desert in March. This had blown great clouds of dust over the Alps and onto the glacier. The dark dust absorbed the sunlight and made the ice melt more than usual. The police and forensic experts who arrived on the scene didn't realize the body was so old. They hacked it out of the ice (above) and flew it by helicopter to Innsbruck, Austria, to be examined. At first it seemed that he was Austrian, and Austria has become the center of Iceman research. But surveyors later found that the body had lain just inside the modern Italian border.

RADIOCARBON DATING
Robert Hedges works at the Radio-carbon Unit at Oxford University in England. He developed a new method of radiocarbon dating, which he used to prove that the Shroud of Turin (far right) was a fake. Radio-carbon dating works because all organic (living) things contain a molecule called carbon-14. This disappears at a constant rate after they die. So by measuring the level of carbon-14, scientists can calculate the age of any organic substance. Hedges dated the Iceman by testing a small bone sample. His results shocked experts, who had guessed that the Iceman had died around 2000 B.C.

SHROUD OF TURIN
People once believed that the body of Christ was wrapped in this relic. But radiocarbon tests showed that it was made in the Middle Ages.

Part of leather shoe lined with grass, still stuck on foot

Leather quiver   Wooden ax with copper head

ARMS AND THE ICEMAN
Some of the items the Iceman was carrying are extraordinary. There was a bow and a leather quiver holding 12 half-made arrows. His ax looks like a typical Bronze Age model from about 2000 B.C., but it turned out to be copper. It is an amazing tool, much older and more advanced in design than any known copper ax.

BACK ON ICE
Once he had been removed from the glacier, the Iceman began to thaw and was in danger of decaying. A fungus had already started to spread across his body. Austrian medical experts removed this with great care. Then they refroze the body in a giant refrigerator at 21°F (–6°C).

GOOD HEAD OF TEETH
Examination of the Iceman's teeth showed that he was probably in his late twenties when he died. His teeth are badly worn, probably from a lifetime of eating coarse grain.

FROZEN IN TIME
So who was the Iceman? He was at least 5 ft 2 in (1.57 m) tall and had several strange tattoos. He was once well dressed for the mountains in patched leather clothes and shoes stuffed with grass for extra warmth. He also had a grass bag and cape. He was carrying an ax, a bow and arrows, and a flint scraper in a leather pouch, which may have been a kit for starting fires. What was he doing with all this gear so high in the mountains? He may have been a hunter or a traveler from a farming town on a trading mission. It is not clear in what direction he was crossing the Alps. He may have come from one of several known towns in Italy, Austria, or southern Germany.

Bog mummies

SOME ANCIENT BODIES have been found in wet, marshy places such as bogs. They are often found by people cutting peat (decomposed plant matter that has been burned as a fuel for centuries). The discovery of a body in a bog usually attracts the attention of the police, who assume that someone has had an accident or been murdered recently. Only after the body has been radiocarbon dated (p. 56) can scientists tell how long ago the person died. The best bog mummies have been found in northern Europe, especially Denmark. They date from the late Iron Age, as early as 500 B.C., to the Roman period, up to A.D. 400. These well-preserved corpses have a number of things in common, and archaeologists believe they are from a similar culture. The victims were all killed on dry land and then thrown into the bog. They may have been executed as punishment for some crime, or as a human sacrifice to the gods. Their many injuries even suggest that the victims were executed in some religious ritual. Forensic evidence suggests that they all died in midwinter, so this may have been a festival celebrated at that time.

LINDOW WOMAN
In 1983, two peat workers stumbled upon a partly decomposed female head in the same bog in Cheshire, England where Lindow Man (p. 59) was later found. A local man soon confessed that he had murdered his wife and dumped her in the bog 23 years earlier. He was tried and found guilty of murder. But when the head was radiocarbon dated, it was found to be over 1,770 years old!

Severed arm

HULDRE FEN WOMAN
This bog woman was found over 100 years ago in Huldre Fen in Denmark. She died about A.D. 95. Most bog bodies are naked, but she was wearing a lambskin cape and a checked skirt and head-scarf. A finely crafted horn comb and a string with two amber beads were also found with her. This suggests that she was not poor and may have held an important position in society. No one knows if her arm was cut off before or after she died.

The hair of many mummies seems to have turned red over the years

Scar from cut throat

GRAUBALLE MAN
This body of a man was found near Grauballe, Denmark, in 1952. At first he was thought to be a drunken peat worker known as Red Christian, who had fallen into the bog way back in 1887. But he is now known to have died between 1,540 and 1,740 years ago. After it had been taken out of the bog, the body had to be treated to stop it from deteriorating. It was placed in a strong solution of oak bark and slowly tanned over 18 months. Grauballe Man is incredibly well preserved, with most of his internal organs intact. Even his fingerprints could be studied (p. 49). The contents of his stomach told scientists what he had eaten for his last meal. He seems to have had a vegetable soup which contained barley and a sort of muesli made from the seeds of over 60 different plants. He died violently, from many injuries, including a cut throat.

Long, narrow hand

Leathery skin, naturally tanned in peat bog

OVERKILL
Lindow Man seems to have been killed by several methods. A knotted cord was found embedded in his neck. It seems to have been used to choke or strangle him. His throat was also cut, and his skull was caved in by heavy blows. All this "overkill" suggests that his death was a sacrifice or some kind of religious ceremony.

Fragile hair, including a beard, rarely found on bog bodies

Cord used to choke or strangle him

AGREEING ON A DATE
Bogs contain little oxygen. This stops bacteria, which cause decay, from growing (p. 8). How well a body is preserved also depends on how cold the water is and how deeply the body is submerged. A team of archaeologists and other specialists removed Lindow Man from the peat. They then took samples from the body and the peat and sent them to three research laboratories to be dated by the radiocarbon method. Though their results were not identical, the experts eventually agreed that the Lindow Man had died around 300 B.C.

Ulna, one of the bones in the forearm

Fingernail resting on skin

Fragments of bones from right hand

Navel

Tough, leathery skin

WHAT DID HE LOOK LIKE?
Lindow Man must have looked a lot better 2,300 years ago. But his face was distorted over the centuries as he lay crumpled in his wet grave. This was a challenge for scientists who try and reconstruct faces to help the police to identify human remains. They based their calculations on careful measurements of the skull, allowing for the thickness of skin and muscle. The fine condition of his fingernails shows that Lindow Man didn't work with his hands, and may even have been a chieftain.

Lindow Man

In 1984, peat cutters found a man's body in a bog at Lindow Moss in Cheshire, England. The discovery that he was about 2,300 years old made the dead man famous overnight. Newspapers gave him the nickname Pete Marsh, a pun on the type of bog he was found in. Scientific research revealed many interesting details about his body. Examination of his teeth suggests he was between 25 and 30 years old when he died. He was in good health, but suffered from intestinal worms. The contents of his stomach showed that his last meal was a high-fiber mixture of cereal, bran, and slightly burnt bread.

The mummies of Sicily

ABOUT 6,000 MUMMIES are still resting in a catacomb (underground cemetery) beneath a Catholic church in Palermo, the capital of the Italian island of Sicily. The first mummies, nearly 400 years old, are of monks who lived and worshiped in the church. The custom soon became fashionable with doctors, lawyers, and other rich professionals in Palermo. The monks embalmed the bodies themselves, in a secret process that took more than a year. Like the ancient Egyptians, the Sicilians didn't find their mummies disturbing. They saw the preserved bodies as a direct link with their dead relatives, whose spirits were enjoying the afterlife. Families took their children to visit their great-grandparents, long after they had passed away. Visitors brought picnics on their outings to the catacombs. The families would pray and talk to the mummies, keep them up-to-date on local affairs, and ask their advice on difficult matters. No one has been mummified here for over 70 years, but the monks are still kept busy giving tours to visitors.

FOUNDING FATHER
The oldest mummy in the catacombs is Father Silvestro da Gubbio, embalmed in 1599. First, his body was carried down to a special cellar, the *collatio*. Here it was laid on earthenware pipes and left for 12 months, until all the body fluids had drained away. It was then taken upstairs and left to dry in the sunshine. Before it was dressed, the body was washed in vinegar and wrapped in straw and sweet-smelling herbs.

BEARDED GUARDIANS
The monks live over the catacombs and are in charge of the mummies and all the cemetery records. They belong to the Capuchin order. All Capuchin monks have beards and wear robes with hoods.

DRESSED IN SUNDAY'S BEST
These mummies of women are all from a part of the catacombs known as the Corridor of the Virgins. Their costumes are a remarkable historical record of dress-making skills and textile design. The lacework is particularly impressive. The coffins the bodies lie in are hinged, so relatives could hold hands with the mummies while they prayed.

Well-preserved, colorful clothes

Labels with details like the dead person's name, age, and profession

MILKY SOFT
In the 19th century, a new, better method of embalming was developed. The monks began to soak the bodies in arsenic or milk of magnesia, which left the skin softer and more lifelike.

DUSTY DEATH
There are now fewer than 40 monks looking after the 6,000 mummies. Every year, they give the dead bodies a gentle clean with a vacuum cleaner.

Clothes of cotton, which has worn less than silk

Sicilian mummy with head propped up on pillow

SLEEPING BEAUTY
Rosali Lombardo, the last Sicilian to be mummified, died at the age of two in 1920. Her body was preserved by a unique process developed by her father, who was a doctor.

Other mummies

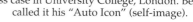

Natural mummies are preserved by accident (pp. 8–9), and are found anywhere in the world where it is cold, dry, or marshy enough. Australian aborigines, Torres Strait Islanders, and native South and North Americans all used natural conditions to preserve bodies deliberately. In Christian churches and Buddhist temples, holy people are sometimes mummified and put on display (pp. 7, 60–61). Every year, the mummy of a Christian saint is carried through the streets in a great procession in a town in Crete. In the 20th century, people have begun to mummify famous politicians and celebrities rather than kings and saints. Improved methods of embalming involving paraffin wax were developed in Argentina. In 1952, these were used to preserve beautifully the body of the president's wife, Eva Perón. In Salt Lake City, Utah, you can now pay to have a dead relative or pet embalmed and wrapped in the ancient Egyptian way.

GUANCHE MUMMIES
In 1770, a volcanic cave containing about 1,000 mummies was found on Tenerife, one of the Canary Islands. They belonged to the Guanche people, who had been preserving their dead for centuries. Their method of embalming was remarkably like the Egyptian way. In some cases the Guanches removed the internal organs. Then they dried the body and stuffed it with plants. Few Guanche mummies have survived, because so many were ground up for medicines in the 16th century (p. 40).

Wax head

Real head

AUTO ICON
When the English philosopher Jeremy Bentham died in 1832, he left his body to a surgeon friend. According to his instructions, his head was mummified. His skeleton was then dressed in his everyday clothes and crowned with a wax head. The whole ensemble is still displayed in a glass case in University College, London. Bentham called it his "Auto Icon" (self-image).

FISHY MUMMY
Mermaids (and, more rarely, mermen) were popular curiosities in Europe as early as the 17th century. These imaginary creatures mostly came from East Asia, especially Japan. This mummified merman was made from a monkey's body and a fish's tail. Seijiro Arisuye, who gave it to an English prince, claimed that it had been caught by a Japanese fisherman.

Sealskin trousers

Outer parka made of sealskin trimmed with fur

Kamik, sealskin boots

LADY DAI, HER TRUE STORY

Lady Dai was a Chinese noblewoman from the Han dynasty who died around 168 B.C. Her well-preserved body was found in a deep tomb in Hunan province in 1972. She was wrapped in 20 layers of silk and lay in a nest of six wooden coffins, all beautifully painted. These were covered in many layers of bamboo matting and five tons of charcoal. This was probably designed to soak up any water and keep the body perfectly dry. The tomb was then sealed with dirt and clay to keep it airtight. Examination of her body showed that Lady Dai had been embalmed by soaking in a bath of mercury salts.

Lady Dai being X-rayed

2,160 pieces of nephrite, a kind of jade, linked with gold wires

SUN-DRIED
This New Guinean is posing proudly with a mummified ancestor. In hot parts of the world, many people used to place bodies in the branches of trees to be dried by the sun. The islanders of the Torres Strait, between Australia and New Guinea, would tie a dead body to a bamboo stretcher. Then they would light a fire under it and smoke it dry. Finally they painted the body with red ocher.

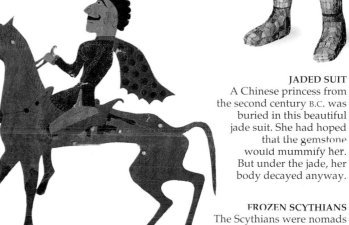

JADED SUIT
A Chinese princess from the second century B.C. was buried in this beautiful jade suit. She had hoped that the gemstone would mummify her. But under the jade, her body decayed anyway.

FROZEN SCYTHIANS
The Scythians were nomads who ruled central Asia from the seventh to the third century B.C. They mummified their dead chiefs and nobles with as much care as the ancient Egyptians. They removed the internal organs and stuffed the body with frankincense, parsley, and hair. This picture of a Scythian horseman is part of a textile buried with a chief. The Scythians spent most of their lives on horseback, and chiefs were even buried with their mummified horses. Warriors were tattooed for their bravery, and one chief has elaborate tattoos all over his body. Their burial mounds in Siberia were freezing cold, which helped to preserve the bodies.

DRESSED IN FURS
This mummy of an Inuit (Eskimo) woman is one of eight well-preserved bodies found in Greenland in 1972 (p. 7). She died around 1475 at the age of 30. The combination of dry air and freezing temperatures naturally freeze-dried her body. Her warm clothing, handmade from animal skins, was also well preserved. The Inuit believed that a dead person's soul would need warm clothes for the long voyage to the land of the dead. Infrared photographs revealed faded tattoos on her face. Four of the other five women buried with her had similar tattoos.

Inner parka made of bird skin

Index

Acknowledgments

Dorling Kindersley would like to thank:

The staff of the Department of Egyptian Antiquities, British Museum, London, in particular John Taylor & Carole Andrews; Ian Mackay at the Museum of Mankind, London; Angela Thomas and Arthur Boulton of the Bolton Museum; John Saunders, Stephen Hughes, and the staff of the Department of Medical Physics, St. Thomas' Hospital, London (p. 51); Reg Davis; Don Brothwell; Joyce Filer; Guita Elmenteuse; George Bankes at the University of Manchester; Theya Molleson at the Natural History Museum, London;

the Seventh Earl of Carnavon; the Egypt Exploration Society; Nicholas Reeves; William and Miranda MacQuitty; Peter Nahun; Martin Davies; Maria Demosthenous; Mitsuko Miyazaki in Japan; Martin Atcherley in Germany; Michael Dunning and Geoff Brightling for additional photography; Gillie Newman for illustrations on pp. 10 & 15; James Putnam for the illustration on p. 25; Belinda Rasmussen; Helena Spiteri for editorial help; Sharon Spencer and Manisha Patel for design help; Céline Carez for her enthusiastic research.

Index: Judith Ann Smith

Picture credits
a=above, b=below, c=centre, l=left, r=right
Ancient Art and Architecture Collection: 56cr; Ardea, London Ltd: 23ac, /Akelindau: 13br; /John Mason: 44bc; /Peter Steyn: 45ar; Owen Beattie/University of Alberta: 9br; British Museum: 23al, 28al, 29al, 29br, 31br, 31ac, 34ar, 44ar, 59al, 59ar, 62bl; /Robert Harding Picture Library: 11br; Jean-Loup Charmet: 36al; Chief Constable of Cheshire: 58al; Christopher Cormack/Impact: 60al, 60ar, 60c, 60b, 61l, 61ar, 61cr, 61br; Reg Davis: 49al, 50al; C. M. Dixon: 63c; Egyptian National Museum, Cairo /Giraudon /Bridgeman Art Library, London: 38cl; Egypt Tourist Office: 15bc; Electa, Milan: 6cr; E. T. archive: 29al; Mary Evans Picture Library: 14ar, 17br, 29bcl, 36bl, 39c, 40al, 41cl; Forhistorisk Museum, Moesgard: 58b; Ronald Grant Archive: 40bc; Griffith Institute, Ashmolean Museum, Oxford: 24al, 35cb, 38br; Hammer Film Productions/Advertising Archives: 41al; Robert Harding Picture Library: 11al,

29acl, 38bl, 38c, 38ar, 39al, 39ar, 39br, 55al, 63ar; Michael Holford: 7cr, 29ac, 55ar; Hulton-Deutsch Collection: 16bl, 26br, 47cr; Louvre, Paris/Bridgeman Art Library, London: 11cr, 42al, /Giraudon/Bridgeman Art Library, London: 13ar, /Photo R.M.N: 10cl, 25al, 42bl; MacQuitty Collection: 7br, 10ar; Manchester Museum, University of Manchester: 48b; Mansell Collection: 6ar, 10bl; Musée de l'Homme, Paris: 54br; Museum of London: 9bl; National Museum, Copenhagen: 58ar; National Museum, Greenland: 7c, 62-63b; Oldham Art Gallery, Lancs/Bridgeman Art Library, London: 43bc; Paramount Pictures: 41tr; Pelizaeus-Museum, Hildesheim: 10tc, 12br, 14b; Popperfoto: 55c; Rex Features Ltd: 6cl, 56bl, 56c, 57ar, 63acl; Photo R.M.N: 27c; Silkeborg Museum, Denmark: 9cl; Sygma: 36br, 38al, 50ar, 51bl, 56al, 57al, 56-57b; University College, London: 62ar, Collection Viollet 11ar; Xinhua News Agency: 63ac.

1 BIRD
2 ROCKS & MINERALS
3 SKELETON
4 ARMS & ARMOR
5 TREE
6 POND & RIVER
7 BUTTERFLY & MOTH
8 SPORTS

9 SHELL
10 EARLY HUMANS
11 MAMMAL
12 MUSIC
13 DINOSAUR
14 PLANT
15 SEASHORE
16 FLAG

17 INSECT
18 MONEY
19 FOSSIL
20 FISH
21 CAR
22 FLYING MACHINE
23 ANCIENT EGYPT
24 ANCIENT ROME

25 CRYSTAL & GEM
26 REPTILE
27 INVENTION
28 WEATHER
29 CAT
30 BIBLE LANDS
31 EXPLORER
32 DOG

33 HORSE
34 FILM
35 COSTUME
36 BOAT
37 ANCIENT GREECE
38 VOLCANO & EARTHQUAKE
39 TRAIN
40 SHARK

41 AMPHIBIAN
42 ELEPHANT
43 KNIGHT
44 MUMMY
45 COWBOY
46 WHALE
47 AZTEC, INCA & MAYA
48 BOOK

49 CASTLE
50 VIKING
51 DESERT
52 PREHISTORIC LIFE
53 PYRAMID
54 JUNGLE
55 ANCIENT CHINA
56 ARCHEOLOGY

57 ARCTIC & ANTARCTIC
58 BUILDING
59 PIRATE
60 NORTH AMERICAN INDIAN
61 AFRICA
62 OCEAN
63 BATTLE
64 GORILLA, MONKEY & APE

65 MEDIEVAL LIFE
66 FARM
67 SPY
68 RELIGION
69 EAGLE & BIRDS OF PREY
70 WITCHES & MAGIC-MAKERS
71 SPACE EXPLORATION
72 SHIPWRECK